Every village or town has a name. We use them every day, even though most were created at least 1,300 years ago. Yet, until now, we knew little about how these names were given and even less about the people who originally used them.

The innovative research in *Surrey Place-names* brings to life this little-known era of the past, the so-called 'Dark Ages' when Britons and Anglo-Saxon peoples coexisted and arrangements for administering the land evolved. Gavin Smith shows that geography is key to understanding these arrangements as river crossings, soil types and the need for trade at recognised places are all important. His work reveals that many parishes reflect patterns established in the Iron Age.

There were many influences on the naming of Surrey's places: early paganism, multicultural mixing, economic development, land management, ecclesiastical history, regional politics, the influence of London, and a gradual shift from Celtic to the Old English language. *Surrey Place-names* unravels these complex influences for the first time and reveals hitherto unknown aspects of the county's history.

Gavin Smith was born and brought up in Surrey. He is a geographer by training and a long-standing member of the Surrey Archaeological Society and the Surrey Wildlife Trust.

SURREY PLACE-NAMES

Gavin Smith

Heart of Albion

SURREY PLACE-NAMES

Gavin Smith

Cover illustration by Gavin Smith

ISBN 1 872883 84 2

Published by

Heart of Albion Press
2 Cross Hill Close, Wymeswold
Loughborough, LE12 6UJ

albion@indigogroup.co.uk

Visit our Web site: www.hoap.co.uk

Printed in England by Booksprint

Contents

List of illustrations

MAPS

PHOTOGRAPHS

Acknowledgements

I have first to acknowledge my own history, since it is bound to have influenced my findings. Born and watered in Reigate, I have lived and worked in London, Sheffield, the Lake District, Norfolk and now Bristol. All these experiences have revealed to me how different Surrey is, but how connected also. Difference and connectedness necessarily are amongst my themes.

I have to thank too, mostly for challenging commentaries on earlier drafts: Richard Coates of the English Place-Name Society, Dennis Turner of the Surrey Archaeological Society, Rob Poulton and David Bird of Surrey County Council's Archaeology Unit, John Blair of The Queen's College Oxford, Jeremy Harte of the Bourne Hall Museum in Ewell, and my good friend and Londoner Alby Stone. Versions of my chapters on *ingas, ge, leah* and on the adoption of English in Surrey have appeared in the *Bulletin* of the Surrey Archaeological Society during 2003–5, for which my thanks to editor Phil Jones. Thanks too, to Bob Trubshaw for organizing the production of this volume and to Anne Tarver for drawing the maps.

I alone am responsible for any and all errors.

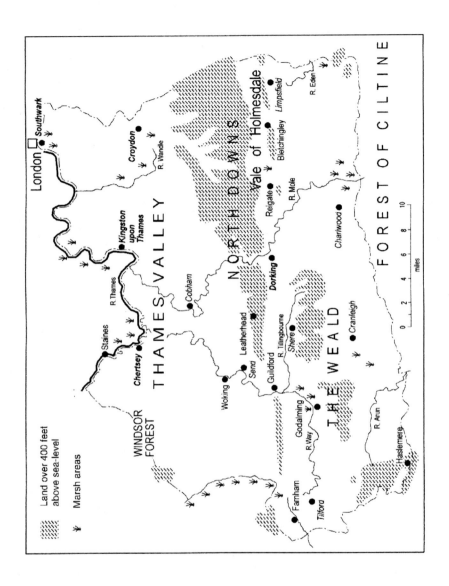

Figure 1: The Surrey landscape.

Key to fonts used for place-names:

Woking: *Medieval market town*

Tilford: *One of the twelve typical names discussed in this book.*

Croydon: *Both of the these categories.*

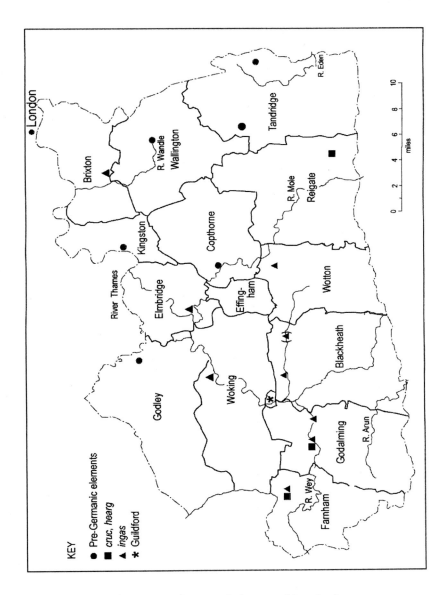

Figure 2: Early central places and hundreds.

Pre-Germanic elements: Caterham, Chertsey, Croydon, Leatherhead, Limpsfield, London, Waleport (Kingston).

cruc, hearg: *Crooksbury, Crutchfield, Peper Harow.*

ingas: *Bintungom (Binton), Dorking, Eashing, Getinges (Eaton), Godalming, Tooting, Tyting, Woking.*

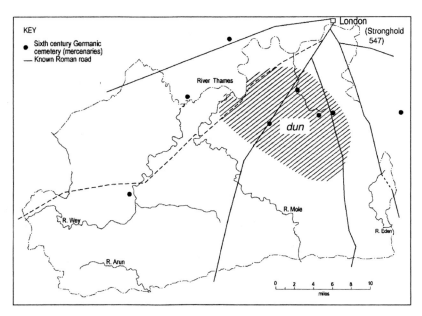

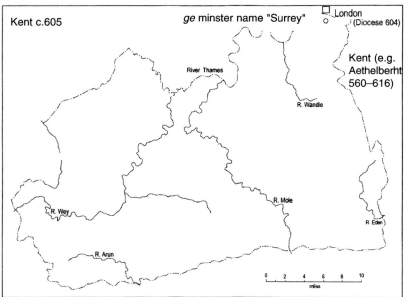

Figure 3: The dominant powers

Top *Figure 3a: City-state of London, c.550*

Bottom *Figure 3b: Kent c.605*

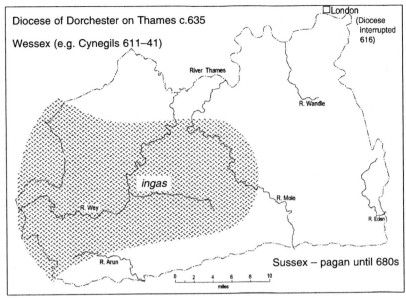

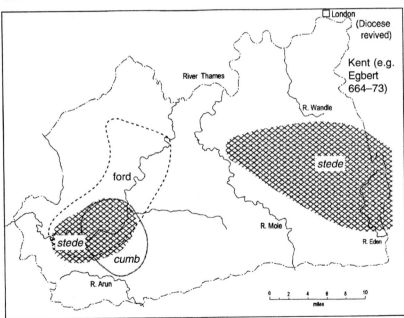

[Figure 3: The dominant powers, cont.]

Top *Figure 3c: Wessex and Northumbria, c.640*

Bottom *Figure 3d:* Kent, c.660

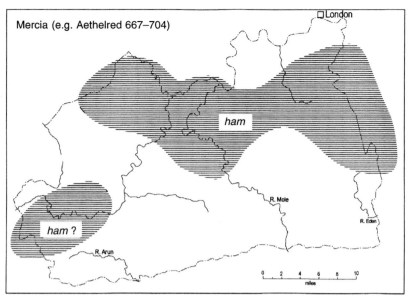

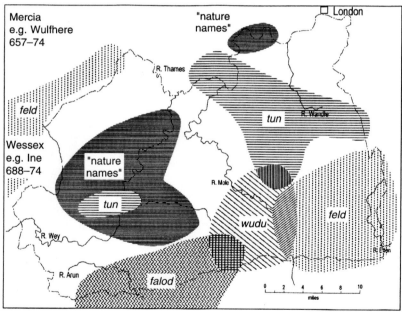

[Figure 3: The dominant powers, cont.]

Top *Figure 3e: Mercia, c.675.*

Bottom *Figure 3f: London the metropolis, c.700 onwards*

FOR STARTERS

1. Introduction

This book attempts something different in the interpretation of Surrey's place-names. For example the English Place-Name Society's standard volume *The Place-Names of Surrey* (1934) told us that the name of **Shere** is an Anglo-Saxon word meaning 'bright' – presumed to refer to the clear waters of the River Tillingbourne. It failed to mention that the name has transferred a mile from its source at the Silent Pool, formerly Shirburn Spring, and why.

Place-Names omits also that **Kingston upon Thames** appears to have had at least two previous names, Moreford and Freoricburna. And possibly a third, Waleport. This last is 'Britons' town'; its second element (*port*) being derived from Romano-British Latin.

I have therefore tried to dig a little deeper. I have reasoned that if we examine a dozen archetypal Surrey place-names (they are located on Figure 1, see page viii), they might reveal something about 'Roman Britain' and 'Anglo-Saxon England'. They might speak too of our social structures, and our conversion to Christianity. We might learn about changes to our landscape and its ecology, and about trade. We might also expose some of the political upheavals behind place-name changes, associated with the slow spread of the English language across the county.

I started this research because I wanted to know who made 'my' native landscape. In practice, this book can be read as a detective story, because that is how I have approached it.

All writers are biased, present company not excepted. A geographer by training, my first love is maps. Thus it comes as no surprise that my path into the maze of place-name studies relies heavily on observable patterns of place-names. Take a look at the maps shown in Figure 3. *Place-Names* noticed some of these patterns in 1934; its endpaper had a pocket containing intriguing charts of place-name distributions. Of how *ingas* names like **Dorking** occur along Surrey's rivers (or is it along

1

Roman roads?). How *ham* names like **Cobham** are concentrated in the northern half of the county, unlike *stede* names of the type **Oxted** which fall mostly in the east. *Leah* names (**Cranleigh**, **Purley**, etc.) occur all over, and so on. Until now, these patterns have never been satisfactorily explained.

My path has taken me into political history and strayed productively into ecclesiastical history, archaeology, anthropology, ecology. Answers then emerged which are very different from those of *Place-Names*, or indeed from modern standard works like Margaret Gelling and Ann Cole's *The Landscape of Place-Names*, 2000, or the English Place-Name Society's new tome published by the University of Cambridge.

A major finding is that many of our place-names aren't 'English' at all. At least, not in the accepted sense.

The index is relatively comprehensive. At the last count it contained 89 Old English place-name elements, the names of 35 Dark Ages persons, 152 subject-matters for everything from 'abandoned sites' to 'yew-trees', and 321 Surrey place-names. The intention is that the index can guide you around the book, and follow subjects of interest. For the same reason, where a specific Surrey place-name is discussed it is highlighted in **bold text**.

2. How do place-names work?

This chapter is about theory, because without a theory as to how our place-names come about, we have little chance of grasping a name's meaning. And until now, it could fairly be said that the evidence offered by Surrey's early place-names was still largely waiting to be de-coded.

Early place-names are our principal documentary evidence from what are colloquially called the Dark Ages. That obscure period falls between the departure of the Roman legions and the re-establishment of a more or less centralized state whose Christianity is exemplified by the writings of Bede, the 'founder of English history'. In essence, the period 400 to 700 AD. But, since part of my purpose is to make these ages less dark, I shall not use the term again.

Models and paradigms

In the theory of science, 'paradigms' are the assumptions underlying any given piece of research. Often they are unstated. 'Models' are more detailed reasonings made beneath the shelter (or sometimes shadow) of an umbrella paradigm.

Until now, what might be called a 'colonial migration' paradigm has been in force in place-name studies. Thus it has been commonplace to assume that Anglo-Saxons arrived in southern England in the fifth century, dislodged the Romano-Britons (turning them into the Welsh), set about colonizing the forested, effectively empty landscape and, working in patriarchal bands, invented our Old English place-names. These names, supposedly, reflect features of aforesaid empty landscape. Is this paradigm realistic? Well, not necessarily.

The landscape was far from empty, though a typical physical geographer's map like Figure 1 might imply that at some point it was. Yet notice how neatly Surrey's towns fit into the structure. Even after the Romans left, Britain was one of the more intensively farmed landscapes of Europe. Romano-Britons did not disappear, they simply were no longer in charge; or if they were, made a point of resembling Anglo-Saxons (rather as before, they had tried hard to resemble Romans). We are talking cultural change, and only to a lesser extent racial or economic change. Economic change had occurred earlier, in late Roman times, with the widespread collapse of the Roman industrialized command economy. The relatively small proportion of in-coming Anglo-Saxons, more in East Anglia than Surrey, were good at adapting to the new circumstances. They became the new cultural leaders, often with the help of a bit of arm-twisting along the way.

These are my paradigms for Surrey at the end of the Roman era, which may be different from yours. I have borrowed them from the likes of Nicholas Higham and the late John Morris. They cannot be proven (though archaeologists are busily gathering the evidence), but let us for the moment assume they *might* be true. It will be a fruitful exercise.

Place-name analysis

So, to the basics. When trying to work out what an early place-name means, a number of questions have to be asked. What was it originally the name of? Who named it; when, and why? Has it perchance *moved*? What, indeed, language is it in? And can surrounding place-names assist us in arriving at a sensible interpretation, after this lapse of one and a half millennia?

To understand how such questions might be answered, and whether they even can be answered, take the example of **Richmond upon Thames**. This clearly is Norman-French, and English, and Celto-Latin: Richemont / upon / Tamesis. Initially the name of a palace, this town name was invented (because Richmond was once **Sheen**) by King Henry VII some time after 1485. He borrowed it from his previous title the Earl of Richmond, relating to Richmond Castle in Yorkshire, itself named after one of the Richemonts in Normandy. This place-name has thus moved (not counting the move from Normandy to Yorkshire) approximately 180 miles.

Now, using our revised paradigms, try a genuinely early example, **Limpsfield**. This names a village, a parish and a church in the Vale of Holmesdale below the Downs of east Surrey. As it happens this place-name isn't English either, or only partly so, since its first-element is a Celtic word for 'elm-trees'. And once again it probably has moved – perhaps two or three times. The 'Limp' part may originally (I say 'may' because place-name detection is rarely certain) have named the Romano-British temple and villa a mile away in Titsey Park. The temple looks to have been centred upon a sacred spring called after its issuing river (now our **River Eden**, named after Edenbridge in Kent).

The river was named presumably from economically-useful elm-trees (Celto-Latin *Lemonum*) that once lined its banks. The river, one supposes, was named by nearby British communities before the Romans arrived. All this is guesswork, but not unreasoned guesswork.

Subsequently the Romano-British estate name 'Limp' acquired an Anglo-Saxon suffix, -*feld* ('field'), which characteristic it shares with a scatter of other parish names in this part of east Surrey in some evidently non-random way.

So, let's begin to unravel the implications of the various contentions just made. It will take the whole book to do so, but some initial principles can be drawn out.

Estate names

Limpsfield is a parish. This book deals mostly with parish names, which is much the same as saying town and village names. As a very approximate rule, these are our earliest place-names. There is good reason: parish names are the core names of early estates. Usually, these core names came first and have survived; other local names came later and are subsidiary. (Actually this is far from watertight as a model, but it will do).

But what really was 'an estate'? Yes there is the parish: an administrative area which, typically, later acquired a church, a village and sometimes a village green or town market place. But there is also the 'manor'. Medieval manors commonly formed subdivisions of larger parishes, or perhaps equally correctly, were those estates that did not quite become elevated to parish status. Giveaway names for the focus of a manor are farmstead or mansion names of the grander type: 'manor', 'court', 'place', 'house' and more latterly 'park', as at **Great Tangley Manor**, **Old Court Cottage** in Limpsfield (since revealed to be a medieval hall used for the manor's court hearings), **Sutton Place**, **Loseley House**, **Gatton Park**. (The *hlose* of Loseley is said to mean 'pig-shelter', but there may be more to it than that; see the discussion of shambles in Chapter 12). At the smaller scale still, we have the individual farm.

Either the parish, manor or farmstead might have been the 'estate' involved in an early place-name. Yet at a larger scale are other types of estate. Notably the medieval hundred (more on hundreds in Chapter 10), or perhaps an entire forest long gone (we shall meet the Forests of Ciltine, Windsor and Woolmer), or an entire ancient political state or tribe. The city of Leeds seems to be named from a minor state, a British one. So does Dent in Yorkshire, as well as Ripon which seemingly shares the name with Repton in Derbyshire. Some people think '**Surrey**' was the name of a state. But was it?

Central places

The Limpsfield estate (or neighbouring Titsey) must have been some variety of what geographers call a 'central place', a place or estate of above-average importance. After all, it supported a temple and a villa. Yet it does not sit at the centre of a hundred (as we shall find central places usually do); it lies virtually on the boundary with Kent. In fact Titsey-with-Limpsfield is unusual in being a 'failed' or truncated central place. More on these later. When the current Surrey-Kent boundary was established, and indeed dyked, Limpsfield's role seems to have transferred to Westerham, two miles away in Kent (Westerham's name significantly means 'the western *ham*' – presumably, of the state of Kent).

Place-names migrate

A warning: place-names, as already suggested, can move. Shere, I have proposed, moved a mile from Shirburn Spring. 'Limp', probably, moved a mile from Titsey and was succeeded on-site by the name **Titsey**, as 'Shere' was by **Albury** (more on that later). So do not assume that because a place-name is in one place today, it was always there rather than somewhere else. It may have moved when the focus of its estate moved.

Fortunately, names sometimes give themselves away, Shere being a case in point. But not always. **Cobham**, for example, formerly named two adjacent villages Church Cobham and Street Cobham, the two lying within the one parish and now merged to become today's almost-town of Cobham. Which was the original Cobham, we do not exactly know. Nor indeed whether 'Cofa's *ham*' was rather at **Downside** (whose name seems to include ancient *dun*, possibly 'British hill village'), or **Chatley** (where a Roman bath house has been found), or Cobham Court, or **Eaton Farm** (which I cannot find on the map, but which *The Place-Names of Surrey* says preserves the otherwise lost name Getinges, an earlier name for the Cobham estate). All these possibilities lie within the current parish bearing the name Cobham.

With Shere even that's not true, as it is now names the parish next door to that of Albury in which the Silent Pool lies. One has to be careful about location; all is not what it seems. Mostly, we do not know precisely the site originally referred to by a surviving place-name.

Semantics

Of course, the significant question for most readers is: 'What did my particular place-name mean?'

I say 'did mean' because it is in some ways curious that we have forgotten what our place-names are telling us. This fact alone is enough to imply that scribes and dry legal records have long replaced oral transmission as the principle vehicle of place-name and even folklore survival, and that scribes have always been somewhat removed from the general run of people.

The matter is made more difficult because the meaning of a place-name's constituent words may have changed. This is not surprising, as words are always changing their meaning. Think for example of our word 'head'. 'Head' over the last couple of hundred years – even the last 50 years – has had many meanings, some of them rather temporary and reflecting our rapidly changing society and technology. There is no reason to think this much less true for the seventh century, which too was a time of rapid social change (the reason I cite the seventh century will become clear). In this book meaning-changes and variable meanings are given for several place-name elements, including *feld*, *ingas*, *eg*, *llan* and *ford*. Just because we think we know what someone means by the term 'field' today (and we might be wrong), does not prove we know what someone meant by *feld* in the name Limpsfield at a particular date well over a thousand years ago. We don't; we make educated guesses.

As well as the meaning of individual terms, there is also the implication of the name as a whole, and here the whole context can vary, throwing the would-be name detective off the scent. Some place-names referred originally to an object at a given site; others to an area. Thus Shere (or rather Sherbourne, see later) referred to an object, the Silent Pool, which has not moved even though the name has. 'Shere' has evolved to mean an area (a parish) then a different object (the village). The 'Limp' of Limpsfield has gone through even more mutations of meaning, having indicated an object (trees), a different object (a river), a third object (a temple at the river's sacred source),

7

and with its addition –*feld*, an area (the estate, later parish), then a fourth set of objects (the church and village).

Importantly, and far more often than realized, names referred originally to a human *activity* or *function*, rather than to a *site* or *object* as such. The function may be long extinct, or moved away. *Leah* ('-ley') I will suggest denotes a wood's function rather than simply a 'wood' as such. *Wielle* concerns the function of the 'well' in question, rather than a well's mere existence. Such interpretation, admittedly, is out of kilter with current convention in place-name studies, which marries place-name suffixes to particular minutiae of the physical landscape. But the place-naming process in Surrey has over the last 1,500 years been people-centred and community-centred, not landscape-centred.

Whether today's place-names referred originally to an object, area or function is beside the point once a place-name migrates. Place-names that migrate do so usually because whatever their initial meaning, they became the name of an estate, and the name of an estate usually settles upon the current focus of that estate. Today this normally is a village or town.

Old English suffixes

For more detailed examination of place-name processes, histories and meanings we could split this book into individual chapters, each concentrating on the different original types of name, namely those containing the elements '–ley' (*leah*), '-ham' (*ham*), '-field' (*feld*), '-ford' (*ford*), and so on. This book is indeed organized in this manner, as is typical for books on place-name studies. However, most books seemingly ignore the *processes* involved in the naming of places, and if we explore these processes, we may come up with meanings that are different.

For example, we want to know in what way Limpsfield relates to other '-field' names. Obviously this relationship is partly to do with the meaning of the Anglo-Saxon word *feld* (though the likely meaning lies in the economics of rural areas and their management, rather than in a description of areas of 'open ground', as typically stated). Beyond this, we can explore the very real possibility that the occurrence of *feld* is partly, even mainly, to do with *the geography of language change* as this determined how an activity was called by a given term, in a given place and a given time. After all, the namers of Limpsfield could equally well have used *camp* (from Latin *campus*, found not far away in the name **Addiscombe**), or *ersc* (dialect 'ash'; an Anglo-Saxon term meaning ploughed land as in **Wonersh**), or in the Celtic manner the reference to human activity could simply have been left off as in the purely Celtic **Merrow** which translates as 'marly (place/field)'. In the name Merrow, the concepts of 'field' and farming are implied but not stated.

As a general principle, early English place-names conform to a rather limited set of formulae. Most have one of a number of standard suffixes: the *leah, ingas, stede, ham, tun, ford, feld,* etc., that crop up repeatedly. Thus we have Cranleigh, Dorking, Banstead, Cobham, Beddington, Limpsfield, Tilford, whereas Cran, Dork, Ban, Cob, Bed, Limp or Til would look all wrong. We would not recognize them as normal English place-names.

A basic question is: why *was* 'field' added to 'Limp'?

Root names

Suffixes ('second elements' in place-names jargon), while offering useful clues to the linguist (less so to the historian or archaeologist), often are relatively redundant in terms of meaning. In practice, they could have been left off – which is a rather startling.

Look at the evidence. This is difficult admittedly, as most English place-names in their present form have been irretrievably altered by the very processes we are trying to unravel. Yet in some instances such as in Glastonbury we have a name so ancient and so important that significant change is on record. In 744 AD Glastonbury was Glastingei (an *eg* name), but by 732–55 Glestingaburg (a *burh* name). Clearly, the real name – what we might call the 'root name' – is 'Glast', of ancient but uncertain meaning. (More complex arguments might be based on the various names of St Albans, whose versions in Bede display *three* alternative roots, based on the unexplained Romano-British 'Verulam', an early abbot Wacol, and the saint himself, respectively).

A root commonly is found as first-element. In Limpsfield's case, 'Limp'. If we concentrate on this root (visible in purer form in Limpsfield's earliest record Limenesfelde in the Domesday Book), we immediately realise it recurs elsewhere – in the east Kent town names Lyminge and Lympne, both derived from a lost name for the River Rother, with Lympne the Romano-British town Portus Lemanis as recorded in 4 AD in a Roman road itinerary. Identical are the river-names Leam and Lemon elsewhere in England, Leven in Scotland, and indeed Lac

Leman (Lake of Geneva) on the French-Swiss border. Who would have thought it – Limpsfield takes its place in the wider world of European place-names.

Our last language change?

Seen in this light Surrey's place-names assume a more 'Welsh' aspect. While English place-names show an odd preference for a stilted set of twiddly-bits (the *ham, feld,* etc.), Welsh place-names tend to be 'nature names': names more like Surrey's **Ash** ('ash-tree') and **Byfleet** ('by the river') that don't have the expected English suffixes. The fiddly-twiddlies that we place-name anoraks lavish so much attention upon are to a great extent linguistic affectations – semantic redundancies. They exist *because of the change from Celtic to English*, and are absent in Wales because there the language did not change.

It goes without saying that these are radical statements, and it is necessary to justify them.

We are not as 'English' as we think. By similar token, our English language is not a given. Our penultimate national language, Celtic, keeps bubbling up through the place-name record, as Limpsfield shows.

We can go further. The study of place-name patterns offers invaluable evidence of how, when and where the English language came gradually into dominance. Only by chance is Surrey not today speaking Latin (in the fourth century we almost did), Danish (Alfred the Great blocked that in the ninth century) or French (Henry the Fifth made a political virtue of scuppering Norman-French during the Hundred Years War; though it still survives in legal and military parlance).

Place-names are a clue to our shifting concepts of national self. It is not clear yet whether the inhabitants of Surrey will be speaking American English by the end of the twenty-first century and perhaps somewhat later, Mandarin Chinese. The issue is that of cultural leadership.

Political history

Talk of kings and wars might sound a trifle old-fashioned. Not so. The ebb and flow of history is not to be dismissed.

During the course of this book we will need to make swift forays into Surrey's history. Surrey, lying alongside the Thames, was close to the very crucible of national development. At various times during the seventh century it was overrun by Wessex, Kent, Mercia, then Wessex again. In terms of ecclesiastical politics Surrey seems likely to have been within the diocese of London from 604 AD, but later was transferred into that of Winchester (and later again, Southwark).

For one brief moment Surrey was at the heart of national events. Both Bede and the *Anglo-Saxon Chronicle* report the life of a royal Celtic-named pagan Caedwalla who emerges from hiding in the Wealden forests, takes Sussex (a minor independent kingdom), and is converted to Christianity by Wilfrid, bishop at Selsey. During a short reign of three years in the mid-680s he re-unified Wessex after an era of sub-kings, founded (according to a charter that survives) a minster church at Farnham in Surrey, and defeated Kent. Briefly, he was over-king of all southern England. But at this point he abdicated, went to Rome, saw the Pope and died. Bede thought him splendid, and we shall meet him again.

Did all this seventh-century political turmoil influence the gentle processes of place-naming? You bet. Particularly so, since it coincided with the conversion to Christianity, the re-establishment of relatively stable land-ownership recorded in writing and – most importantly – the change to the English language.

The Church

But by and large it was not kings who named, recorded or remembered place-names. You might think that was left in the hands of the local population, hence the survival of ancient names from other times. But someone else was also involved, or rather another institution. The Church. This has not been fully recognised by students of English place-names.

The Church played three essential roles here. Firstly, two or three generations of redoubtable and holy individuals, subsequently often known as saints, civilized by example the warring kinglets of their times; initially in Ireland and Wales in the fifth and sixth centuries, and in England largely in the seventh. Without this pacifying influence there might have been insufficient social cohesion for place-names to stabilise. Church and kingship were symbiotically tied, since the great majority of ecclesiastics belonged to the same type of families as the kings; they were their brothers and sometimes sisters. No anthropologist would be overly surprised by this; the virile (some would say aggressive) and the thoughtful are different characteristics of social leadership and arise in different individuals, but within the context of particular dominant families or social groupings.

Secondly, the Church was for long the only literate organization and thus in a good position to influence what got written down, including place-names. Most of our earliest place-name records (and a good proportion of later ones) are ecclesiastical land charters.

Thirdly, and as a consequence of its other two roles, the Church was the only body, apart from a few of the grander kings, capable of founding new stable institutions. The possessions and territories of these institutions had to be given names (to the extent that some monasteries were not averse to forging 'original' documents – something historians try to take into account). Necessarily we shall find ourselves contemplating the meanings and considerable influence of the names of monasteries and chapels. This is complicated by the fact that there was more than one 'Church', and that their foundations often were built on pre-existing local religions retaining pre-Christian elements.

The bottom line is that the Church re-established literacy and re-created place-name fixity. A rough rule of thumb is that the Roman Empire created one set of stable economics and stable Celto-Latin place-names throughout England, then there was population and economic collapse, and subsequently the Anglo-Saxon Church created another set of stable place-names, in English but with Celto-Latin survivals. Only relatively minor changes have occurred since, because we have not experienced another language change, or indeed another social collapse.

Fixity

The concept of fixity may be established as a basic principle. Place-names change, or they did, when culture was oral. After our culture became a written one, names changed a lot less. If, that is, a particular name was written down and the scribe did not make too many mistakes (the Domesday Book listing of manors for example shows a tendency to Frenchify the spellings). Which is why so many of Surrey's place-names – again I mean parish or manor names – date from the seventh century. It is my view, admittedly controversial, that this was the century when our major place-names got fixed by the legalistic land-records, especially of Church authorities newly literate at that time. Once a land agent (which the Church undoubtedly was) has hold of a name, they fix it like a butterfly on a card. Nobody is going to risk having their organisation's inheritance challenged as a result of the silly mistake of diverging from the property-name that appears on the card (the card normally being a jealously-guarded ecclesiastical, royal or manorial land-register, some of which survive to this day).

True, sometimes a bit of 'folk etymology' has intruded, for example in the spurious 'guild' of **Guildford** and even more obviously the 'leather head' of **Leatherhead**. Interestingly, in the sixteenth to eighteenth centuries, some scribes developed a democratic habit of recording not only the official (i.e. land registry) version of place-names, but also the local parlance. In 1560 **Epsom** was recorded as 'Ebbisham *alias* Epsham' and in 1592 **Abinger** as 'Abyngworth *alias* Abinger'; but this is unusual and Epsom and Abinger remain irregular in having officially-adopted vernacular forms.

As to why the local populace should themselves have lost sense of the meaning of their own estate names, perhaps this was because they had little use for such names. To them, farm, field, wood, hill, stream and street names perhaps were far more central to their daily lives. These latter names changed many times over the years, probably as circumstances changed. At any one time in history many, perhaps most minor names appear to have been (and indeed to an extent were) modern.

However it would be overstating the case to suggest that *only* parish and manor names survive from earlier times. To a limited extent this is statistically testable. Helpfully, *The Place-Names of Surrey* transcribes several Anglo-Saxon boundary charters including those of Egham-with-Thorpe (a later transcription of a seventh-century original), Farnham Hundred (909 AD), Merstham (947 AD) and Pyrford-with-Horsell (956 AD). Such charter evidence indicates that a third to a half of early minor names may survive to this day (though at Merstham the proportion is tiny), with perhaps another fifth being recorded into late medieval times or beyond. Minor names survived perhaps by means similar to those of estate names: by being recorded by an historically continuous series of land agents, most of whose documentation has since been mislaid but some of which resides in county archives and the like. *The Place-Names of Surrey* illustrates exactly this. Thus for **Farnham** (minster, castle and town) fourteen records are cited between the years 688 and 1228, during which the name shifts from Fernham via Fearnhamme to Farneham. For **Tollsworth**, a farmstead in Chaldon adjacent to Merstham, nine records between 947 and 1402 give Tunles weorth via Tuleswerthe to Tolesworth. These mutations result from scriptural fashion (including the lettering used), scribal error, the evolution of the English language, and inflexions imported from Norman-French.

The hand of land agents in the recording of place-names is perhaps illustrated by names like **Tangley** referring to a *tang* ('tongue') of land, **Horne** (*horn*, 'horn of land'; **Horley** is actually 'the *leah* attached to Horne') and **Hook, Hookwood, Tenningshook** (*hoc*, 'hook of land'), though students have tended to assume such names refer to barely perceptible hill-promontories. There can be no doubt however about **Buckland**; this is *bocland*, 'land held by book or charter' (whereas **Bookham** probably contains *boc*, 'beech'). Some commonplace 'single-element' names clearly defining a site as lying within an assumed wider estate are essentially land agent terminology; into this category might fall **Stoke** (*stoc*, 'subsidiary place'), **Thorpe** (*thorp*, ditto) and a Norman-French example **Capel** ('chapel').

But quite a few lesser names do survive from the seventh century. Thorpe (subsequently a parish) is one, and also from the cited boundary charters can be found a harbour name, **Hythe** in Egham, the *leah* names **Ockley Common** and **Willey,** plus a marsh name **Pudmore** in Farnham Hundred, the river name **Bourne** in Horsell, and so on.

Personal-names in place-names

Similarly, we can explain why numerous estate names (but also some farm names) have fixed to them the personal-names of obscure early inhabitants. Later people get relatively little mention in estate names, the names having been bureaucratically fixed before later comers arrived.

True, place-names ending in *–ingtun* (**Beddington, Addington**, etc.) are thought to date from a little bit later (probably from the later seventh century onwards) and do usually have a personal-name as first element. Were these estates privatised only at that time? Have a new set of owners muscled in on the back of fresh regional conquests? Have ecclesiastical scribes from a different church gained sway? Or were the names transcribed into a new local language? All these options are plausible, and to some extent they overlap. Similar considerations doubtless apply to a number of other place-name suffixes, notably *–worth* (see later). We will find that their geographical distribution patterns offer a way of trying to unravel such complications.

I will have more to say about personal-names later and show that under relatively few circumstances during the last 1,300 years in Surrey has it been advantageous to alter an estate's name by imposing one's own name upon it. The result is that a lot of obscure early personal-names survive. Of course as usual there are exceptions, occurring perhaps when an estate is divided into parts, or when similar common names are in proximity. This we have two Stokes: **Stoke next Guildford**, its Park now famous for the pop festival, and **Stoke D'Abernon**, its church displaying the magnificent brass of Sheriff of Surrey and Sussex Sir John D'Aubernoun, died 1277, complete with lance. Then there is **Tooting Bec**, memorable because I lived there in the early 70s (though it has a connection also with the abbey of Bec in Normany), and **Tooting Graveney**, whom I think was a cricketer. **Temple Elfande** in Capel was in 1263 held by the Knights Templars.

Date and fashion

With place-names there is this question of *date*. Limpsfield is particularly complex. Its first-element is Romano-British (indeed perhaps Iron Age); its suffix Anglo-Saxon and in place by the 880s. How much does this tell us?

It raises the issue of *fashion*. This is a concept little discussed in place-name studies, but crucial. The unstated assumption is that all 'English' place-name suffixes arrived simultaneously. That they were delivered with Hengist and his mob of invading Angles, Jutes and Saxons in the 410s. Well, leave aside that several suffixes including *dun, cumb, ford* seem to be Celtic. Similar words, as I have mentioned, meant different things to different people at different times. Thus it is entirely possible that *ingas* was only used to any great extent in English place-naming during the mid-seventh century, and then (as I shall suggest) only in certain parts of the country. Ditto *ge*, which is even more closely constrained to Kent around 600. *Feld*, as in Limpsfield, seems to have been used initially only in some localities, but gradually changed its meaning and was then applied more widely. And so on. It is anyway generally agreed that *tun*, the quintessential 'English' place-name suffix, came into use only from the later seventh century. We are talking in other words about linguistic fashion, and that is a lot harder to research.

An important part of this book is involved in uncovering specific episodes in these processes. Reference necessarily will be made to the politics of the various states of the Heptarchy (the seven main Anglo-

Saxon kingdoms) and their respective ecclesiastical structures. Their fortunes and fashions did impact upon Surrey place-names.

You have waited too long, so enough theory. Let us move on to the commons and villages that for many are the essence of the Surrey countryside.

EARLY ECONOMICS

3. Cranleigh and the rough commons

The most frequent type of place-name in Surrey (and nearly the commonest parish name) ends in '-ley' or '-leigh', Old English *leah*. For example, **Cranleigh**, **Horley**, **Leigh**, **Ripley**, **Frimley** and many more.

The 'why' part is more difficult. Until now this has not been thought to be a problem, because as *The Place-Names of Surrey* declares *leah* means 'a wood' and Surrey is one the most wooded counties in England. So, no problem. Except that *leah* is said to have meant 'wood' *originally* but later, 'clearing'. Surely, a clearing is the opposite of a wood? In a name like Cranleigh, what is being referred to – the woodlands of this part of the Weald, or perhaps the 'clearing' of Cranleigh's large open green known as Cranleigh Common?

Leah and the common pasture

Rather than 'wood' *per se*, *leah* is likely to mean the *function* of the area in question. In the case of woods, probably it meant what Oliver Rackham (chief authority on the history of woodlands) describes as 'wood pasture '. This is not just playing with words. Woods were used for grazing stock, as can still be observed in Wales or Cumbria today; but woods once over-grazed cease to be woods. Eventually they become grassland or heath. This indeed is thought to have been the major cause of the emergence of Surrey's heathlands, probably during the Bronze Age. Hence an illusory 'sense-progression' (as place-name students call it) from *leah* appearing to mean 'woodland', to *leah* appearing to mean 'a clearing'. More likely, *leah* meant something like *'common grazing-land'*. In effect, *leah* is the forgotten term for Surrey's rough commons. Once we recognize this, we straightway learn a great deal about Surrey's social history and economics.

Della Hooke has reached similar conclusions for the West Midlands, though her preference for 'wood pasture' is perhaps too narrow a definition. The true etymology of *leah* remains uncertain. Pokorny's

survey of Indo-European vocabularies allies it to English 'light'. The semantics of *leah* might thus originally have been anything from '(country with) the light gleaming through (as a result of grazing)' to 'land cleared by fire'. The common theme perhaps is 'grazing land', though the word's roots are so lost in the ancestral European mists that they could as well be Celtic as Germanic.

Wisley, Bisley, Langley, Tangley, Farley, Parley, pudding and pie

As a lad I roamed the commons of Surrey. I knew the woodwarblers and the woodcock amongst the dry scrub-oaks and whortleberries of Wotton Common. I knew the beeches, ash-trees and yews of Ranmore, and the great oaks, the holly trees, the roe buck and the ironstone-laden streams of Holmwood. These were my commons; the wilderness. For me, they make Surrey what it is.

It's in the soil. Surrey is not over-fertile. In fact it is so spectacular in its agrarian unfecundity that Henry II tried to claim almost the whole county as an extension of Windsor Forest so he could hunt it as a deer chase. Although Surrey escaped the fate of afforestation met upon a chunk of similar country in south Hampshire we know today as the New Forest, pudding is the point: the sticky clayey ground of **Cranleigh** Common or of the lost common of **Horley** in the Weald. And pie: the dry dusty sands of the great sweep of **Witley**, **Thursley**, **Ockley** and **Hankley** Commons in far south-west Surrey. No farmer's dream this. But 'wilderness' is not correct, well not these last 3,000 or so years. Because common land by definition is held in common by the community, and *communally managed.* Grazed, hunted, collected over and cropped in ways organized so as to be sustainable. Surrey's first and longest-lasting 'green' economy. But why do I say common grazing land? The rest of this chapter will try to justify this claim.

There are many *leah* names because there are many commons. Surrey's varied soils – clay, sand, chalk – mean many parishes support

---

Opposite: **Reigate Heath.** Heather, bracken, gorse and latterly oak surround the eighteenth-century windmill. This embryonic settlement, if 1,000 years older, might well have been called by one of the typical Surrey place-names **Headley**, **Blackheath**, **Farley** or if more overgrown, **Oakley** or **Oakwood**: from Old English *haeth* ('heather'), *blaec* ('black' or possibly 'bleak'), *fearn* ('bracken') and *ac* ('oak'), combined with *leah* 'grazing common' or *wudu* '(common-land) wood'.

several commons on several different types of unproductive geology. And that *leah* doesn't specifically mean 'wood' is illustrated by names like **Headley** ('heather *leah* '), **Wisley** ('meadow *leah* ') and **Cranleigh** whose long-lost 'cranes' (a huge ostrich-like bird now extinct in England) imply marshy land.

Let the cranes return. Long live the natterjacks, the Dartford warbler, the tree pipit on the heaths, the woodbine in the woods. The old man's beard and the thyme upon the Downs.

If this reads like a love-letter to Surrey's commons, well so it is.

British droving

Leah is first heard in the *Anglo-Saxon Chronicle* for the year 477. The *Chronicle* reports that Saxon invaders landed in Sussex and put the British to flight 'into the wood which is named Andredesleage'. In other words, into the **Weald** of Sussex, Surrey and Kent. The name means 'the *leah* attached to Anderidos', the latter being the Roman name for the massive Saxon Shore fortress still visible at Pevensey. The Weald was 'Wald' in 1235, 'woodland'.

Let us accept for a moment that Andredesleage could mean 'the stock-browsing territory attached to Pevensey'. I suggest that has a parallel in Tenterden in Kent, which relates to the Celtic name of the Isle of Thanet 45 miles distant. The Kentish element –*denn* means something similar to *leah*, and in east Surrey it occurs at a few places including **Stockenden** and **Puttenden**. Andredesleage and Tenterden would seem to be literary evidence for the antiquity of Wealden *stock-rearing and droving* – a practice surviving into the nineteenth century. Are these memories of British tribal land-rights?

There may be other whispers from this ancient folk-world. Chevening in the Vale of Holmesdale in Kent seems to mean 'people below the scarp (of the North Downs)', hung on Celtic *cefn*, 'ridge'. (To see what Britons meant by *cefn*, look at Cefn Bryn, 'ridge hill' a fine ridge across The Gower whose front profile is not unlike the Downs above Holmesdale). Might **Chivington**, a Domesday manor of Blechingley a few miles west in Surrey in the same vale, contain the same term? Again, in the Sussex Weald, East and West Chiltington, 15 miles apart, appear to be a relic of the 'Forest of Ciltine', a name cited alongside that of the Weald as Caedwalla's hiding-place in the 680s. 'Ciltine' is Celtic *celt* meaning 'high' – the same word the Iron Age Celts used of themselves as conquerors. This word names the Chiltern Hills, and in

Sussex presumably once named the Sussex Downs. The Sussex Weald has also two Chiddingly's, likely containing *cet* the Celtic term for 'wildwood' (and perhaps here should be included Chiddingstone in the Kentish Weald).

The impression one gets from this uncertain but cumulative evidence is that the Weald during the upheavals of the post-Roman period was a disparate zone of British tribal re-grouping – a repeat of the pre-Roman withdrawal into the Weald known from archaeology and tentatively associated with the political impacts of Julius Caesar's aborted invasions of 55 and 54 BC. Far from being virgin forest waiting to be colonized by Anglo-Saxon invaders, this large well-treed region woven through with small fertile stream-side meadows and with the tracks of ancestral drove ways, may have been a British redoubt. This is not incompatible with the *Chronicle*'s record of the Weald as hideout for a string of fugitives throughout Anglo-Saxon times. If the Weald *was* essentially British, its economy was stock-rearing, and happy enough in its isolation. Such a perspective fits better the very existence of Celtic-named King Caedwalla and of Liss, a post-Roman designation meaning 'court' or perhaps 'royal court' (Welsh *llys*) just over the Hampshire border. Conceivably, Liss was known to Caedwalla.

Finally, note two large parishes at opposite ends of the Surrey Weald, **Chiddingfold** and **Lingfield**. Both names are open to more than one interpretation but could mean 'fold of the people of the lowland (or perhaps wood)' and 'field of the people of the *leah*' respectively. Might these again refer to ancient folk-groups, and the people British?

In the charts

Two bits of dialect identified by *The Place-Names of Surrey* seemingly describe Surrey's heathlands. One is *ceart*, best known from Chartwell in Kent, but in Surrey appearing at **Churt**, **Hurt Wood** in Shere, **Chart Park** in Dorking, **Limpsfield Chart** and elsewhere. The other is *sceat*, as in **Bagshot** and **Oxshott Heaths**. Apparently the English word 'heath' derives from British *cet*, and I had a fancy both *ceart* and *sceat* might be too: distinct dialect developments arising in long-lived but relatively isolated Celtic-speaking communities, *ceart* along the northern fringe of the Weald, *sceat* around the fringes of Windsor and Woolmer Forests. My linguist colleague however is not encouraging of this notion; he suggests *ceart* might be cognate with English 'yard/garth/garden', which raises the possibility of 'backyard' in some territorial sense (for which see the discussion of 'field' below). In the standard Anglo-Saxon dictionary Clark Hall says *ceart* is known *only* from land charters (giving a definition 'wild common land'); conceivably it is Celtic. *Sceat*, Anglo-Saxon for 'corner/district', might be a landowner's or land agent's term favoured at some era for in-takes around the aforementioned forests (rather as 'Ground' and 'Park' occur on the fringes of Grizedale Forest in Cumbria). For the moment these dialect terms must retain their mystery.

But **Bagshot** is perhaps a parallel to the several Bagley names in other counties, referring to the badger (Bawdrip in Somerset seems to be 'badger trap'). 'Brock' the Badger is one of the very few Celtic words to be absorbed into English; why such interest in them? Were Bagshot's badgers caught for their fur, or are the terrier events at Lakeland Games a clue? The Celts were keen on hunting and war-dogs of all sizes and the business seems to have been adopted with alacrity by Anglo-Saxons and Normans. Henry the Eighth had large parts of north Surrey emparked as a stag-hunting chase convenient for his pads at Richmond, Hampton Court, **Oatlands** ('oat field') and **Nonsuch** ('None such'). All of which puts historical perspective into today's hunting debate.

On ecology

Returning to *leah*, we can check whether it really does mean 'common grazing land' by looking at the *leah* names of the valley of the Old Wey between Shalford and Cranleigh. Of these names, four are associated with small patches of surviving common-land or village greens at **Norley Common**, **Shamley Green**, **Birtley Green** and **Cranleigh Common**. It is reasonable to surmise that the remainder – **Great Tangley Manor, Bramley, Lea Farm**, **Rowly**, **Whipley Manor** – have simply lost their commons. In fact Whipley retains one, called Goose Green, Lea Farm is close to Rushett Common and Tangley could refer to Wonersh Common. The first elements of Bramley and Rowly are respectively 'broom' and 'rough' – fair descriptions of a Surrey common. (Baring-Gould in the nineteenth century wrote a romantic novel entitled *Broom Squire* about the tenuous life-style of smugglers and broom-makers on the west Surrey heaths; brooms made from sprigs of the broom shrubs, that is).

Very minor *leah* names appear already in late Anglo-Saxon charters, so clearly in its end-state *leah* was no longer associated with vast tribal rights but with local administrations. Not uncommonly it becomes paired with what might be called an 'ecological marker' identifying a common's particular characteristic. Bramley and Rowly are examples.

Others are **Farleigh** ('fern' – i.e. bracken), **Birtley** ('birch'), **Bisley** ('bushes'), and **Bently** ('bent-grass'). Broom, bracken, 'roughness', birches, bushes, and bent-grass each mark local stages in ecological successions from woodland to open grass or heath and back again. What the parish names Bramley and Farleigh tell me, plus **Farley Heath** in Albury (on which are the ruins of a Romano-British temple), plus **Farnham** (see below), is that in early Anglo-Saxon times the population crash known to have occurred in England from late Roman times would indeed have resulted in under-grazing and the re-invasion of 'weeds' and denser vegetation.

For an instructive example, look no further than the history of the name **Blindley Heath** near Lingfield. Now a patch of grassland, it was named 'heath' in the sixteenth century, but back in 1365 was referred to as a 'wood called Lynlee'. It must originally have been native lime-wood (a good grazing species), since *lind* means 'lime-tree'. Blindley once was wildwood on the edge of the still partly-wooded zone of south-central Surrey we shall shortly explore. Meanwhile, **Rushett Common** is representative of an etymological speciality of medieval Surrey: vegetation names in a collective '–ett'. Rushet(t) occurs more than once and is 'rushes'; **Ruffet(t)s** are 'rough' scrubland; **Cobbett**, man and farm, I presume refers to small round hard things. Place-names indicative of ecological change continue to arise; for example the various **Juniper Hill** and **Juniper Valley** names on early editions of Ordnance Survey maps mark out the spread of this distinctive evergreen shrub associated with declines in grazing but now (with increased overshadowing by larger trees) again rare in Surrey.

On either side of Reigate town we get a glimpse of the economic activity associated with such changes. To the south lies the manor house of **Kinnersley** (Kinewardslee in 1255). Other instances of Kinner(s)ley occur in Shropshire, Worcestershire and Herefordshire and their first-elements are said to recall persons named Cyneheard or Cyneweard. A safer bet is that they refer to cattle-herders – kineherds or kinewards – who grazed the commons. (By similar token might **Kenley**, again recurring in rough Shropshire, be 'kine-*leah* ' rather than 'Cena's *leah* '?). To the north of the town lies **Colley Wood** (Colelie c.1180). This is 'charcoal-*leah*' and apparently records woodland charcoal-burning a good four centuries before the known late medieval industry of the Croydon area and **Colliers** ('charcoal-burners') **Wood**. Iron Age and Roman Britons were charcoal-burning in the Weald to support their iron-making industries, and we may assume this activity continued.

Hyrst and the woodlanders

So much for the rough grazing-lands, our commons. But wood pasture is only one of the two traditional forms of woodland management identified by Oliver Rackham. The other is coppice, the production of even-sized small timber for a wide variety of construction and manufacturing purposes and for firewood and charcoal, dating from the Stone Age and surviving from that time. Our Atlantic climate suits it. It involves cutting the shoots of hazel and other tree species down to the root stock every seven or so years.

Hitherto no one seems to have suggested a place-name term relating to this widespread practice, except perhaps the *grafa* Gelling and Cole propose. Yet *grafa* is derived from 'graven/dug' and as it presumably indicates an embanked or ditched tree-grown area, could as easily refer to a 'grove' (sacred or otherwise) or orchard. But there is *hyrst*.

Hyrst crops up in parish names at **Crowhurst** ('crow *hyrst*') and **Ewhurst** ('yew *hyrst*') in the Surrey Weald, and is frequent in the names of minor woods and farms scattered thickly across this part of the county and the adjacent Weald of Sussex and Kent. *Hyrst* is said to mean 'wood' or 'wooded hill', but this may not be the whole story. The word derives from the Indo-European root *(s)kera-*, originally 'hair', and more generally 'something that grows' (the Latin derivative was *crinis*, 'hair'). Other derivatives may include our word 'rush' (stuff that grows beside lakes) and more to the point, Old French *brosse* ('brushwood') giving our English word brush(wood) and Welsh *prys*, meaning the same. It is therefore likely that the Anglo-Saxon word *hyrst* also meant 'brushwood', or the sites from which brushwood comes. That is, 'coppice'.

There is also Old English *hris*, 'twig, branch'. *Hris* appears in the minor Surrey place-names **Ricebridge** and **Ridgebridge** where it is paired with 'bridge' in the sense 'causeway' and means 'causeway built of brushwood'. (The old Surrey surname Risbridger presumably means 'brushwood causeway-builder'). Rather as Old Saxon *hros* and Old English *hors* both mean 'horse' and are divergences from the same root, and our word 'grass' in Anglo-Saxon was both *graes* and *gaers*, so *hris* and *hyrst* surely are twins? *Hyrst* may the younger, dialect, version. I surmise both mean aspects of brushwood – either the things made from it or the sites where it is grown.

Certainly *hyrst* is associated with relatively small woodland areas, as is coppicing, and is found in traditional coppicing areas like the Weald and to a lesser extent Epping Forest and the New Forest. Nowadays Wildlife Trusts are reverting to the practice of coppicing as a way of encouraging the springtime carpet of woodland flowers that formerly delighted the eye of the woodlander, and making a bit of money on the side by selling charcoal. Those making the money in medieval and renaissance times were the glass- and iron-masters of the Weald, whose industries required large acreages of coppice, as well as threatening the king's supply of timber for ship-building. From these times date names like **Abinger Hammer** with its one-time water-powered tilt-hammers, and **Furnace Wood** in Chiddingfold.

The village green

When woodland cattle had to be collected to be driven to market for slaughter 'collection points' were needed. In the deep Weald of south-west Surrey and the neighbouring parts of Sussex, these sites were given the name *falod*, '(animal) fold'. Thus the three adjacent villages, **Chiddingfold**, **Dunsfold** ('Dunt's fold') and **Alfold** ('old fold').

Why, if folds were needed here, were they not needed elsewhere? Possibly these 'folds' were what became our village greens – the wide green at Chiddingfold, the winding common at Dunsfold. The term *grene* as 'common, (village) green' dates from medieval times. And were these folds or greens called *feld* at Lingfield in east Surrey, but *denn* at Cowden in Kent? The Weald is full of linguistic localisms; it was a remote and large area in which localisms might survive, especially if communities were cohesive.

A significant presence in the Weald is *plegstow*, 'play place'. Again this could name a village green, as at **The Plaistow** in Lingfield. There are others in Capel and West Clandon, and a whole parish so named in Sussex. The term probably records the mixed religious-secular ceremonies occurring near parish churches and still remembered as such in Ireland. Perhaps their spirit survives best as English village cricket?

Feld and *wudu*

But it is as likely that *feld* had a larger meaning, or several. A field is a field? Not so. Of all the familiar elements in the English place-name toolbox, *feld* may be the most frustrating.

It shows almost no consistency. All Surrey's main *feld* names are concentrated in the south-east of the county (see Figure 3f), but here they display great variation. *Feld* in **Limpsfield**, with its Celtic first-element strictly equivalent to the more famous Lichfield (named from Licced, the lost Roman town of Wall two miles away), might have a meaning equivalent to the Latin *territorium*, 'hinterland'; in other words be another parallel to Andredesleage. **Tatsfield** has a personal-name first-element, whereas **Nutfield** is nuts. According to Eilert Ekwall, both **Linkfield** in Reigate and **Lingfield** appear in Eldorman Aelfred's will of the 870s; meanings must remain doubtful, but Lingfield we have contemplated as an ancient folk-name. Almost the sole feature common to these various names is their geographical bunching, which suggests the shared thread is they all represent a single temporary naming fashion (on a par with the *dun, stede, ingas, ham* and *tun* fashions also mapped in Figure 3 and discussed elsewhere).

This is an interpretation very different from the norm. Gelling and Cole regard *feld* as 'open space in a woodland area', gradually coming to mean our modern 'field'. I prefer Eilert Ekwall's reading: that *feld* in place-names 'probably (was) used in much the same sense as *leah* '. A relevant characteristic again may be *communality*. Was *feld* a communally-managed open area – doubtless initially rough grazing? Far from indicating a forested landscape (as Gelling has argued for the clumps of *feld* parish names in east Berkshire and north-east Sussex), the *feld* parishes of south-east Surrey occur in a territory long civilized. In the locality are at least two Roman villas (in the Vale of Holmesdale), two Iron Age hill-forts (one above the Vale, the other deep in the Weald), and for Surrey a relative abundance of passable farmland and grazing marsh. No sequestered woodland retreat, this.

It seems that by the 870s if not before, estates in south-east Surrey were being extensively *renamed* using the English formula –*feld*. Then a little later again, a set of not nearly so valuable estates further west were renamed into –*wudu*, 'wood'. These are the Wealden parishes of **Charlwood** and **Newdigate** (the latter being either 'the gate into Ewood' or 'the gate into the new wood'), the chapel at **Oakwood**, and in the vicinity the commons of **Holmwood**, **Earlswood**, **Petridgewood**, **Outwood** ('outer') and **Kingswood**. Plus manors or lesser estates named **Ewood** ('yew'), **Shellwood**, **Hartswood**, **Norwood**. Nothing approaching this number of *wudu* names occurs elsewhere in Surrey. In other words, *wudu* is as concentrated in and around the Hundred of Reigate as *feld* is in and around the Hundred of Tandridge (see Figure 3f.). These distributions in no way reflect the pattern of either woods or open space in Surrey as a whole. There are three possible explanations.

The first is purely linguistic: that *leah*, representing communal browsing-lands, was *translated* into 'standard' English as *feld* in one area, but *wudu* in the next. (Note that *leah* does make a good showing in the area, in the parish names **Blechingley, Leigh, Horley**; Ekwall would include **Lingfield**).

The second possibility is that *feld* is the earlier term but that at a later date *wudu* was preferred, *feld* by this time having taken on a different meaning more like its modern one.

Thirdly, Tandridge Hundred with its Roman villas and Iron Age hill-forts always was the most settled part of the Surrey Weald (bar the Godalming-Farnham district; see later) and so really did have more cultivated land and smaller commons, whereas Reigate and Wotton Hundreds to the west remained relatively well-wooded until late. Holmwood (literally 'the home wood', rather like the Home Counties, the wood being closest either to Dorking or conceivably London) was still a royal hunting forest in the seventeenth century. **Wotton** further west again is *wudu tun* .

Quite likely all three of the above propositions are true simultaneously. (And Holmwood gave rise to '**Holmesdale**', as revealed by Daniel Defoe, school-boy in Dorking in the late seventeenth century: 'the vale …. (of) Holm-Wood')

As to semantics, indicative *wudu* names are perhaps Westwood Common (a lost common near Dawes Green), a rare eastern instance **Itchingwood Common** (*aecen wudu*, 'oaken wood') in Limpsfield, and a rare far western instance **Smithwood Common** (a fine name) near Cranleigh; all display *wudu* in its *leah* sense, of '*common grazing.*' Similarly, until the fifteenth century, *feld* appeared in such combinations as Bromfeld, Firsefeld and Honifeld clearly referring to the broom, furze (gorse) and honey-production of *heathland* ; this concurs with the two Hatfield ('heath *feld* ') names that appear in Bede. Terms used in medieval Surrey for what we would understand as a 'field' were rather *aecer* ('acre'), *croft, ersc* (as in Wonersh), *haga* ('enclosure'), *hamm* (see below), *gaerston* ('grassy paddock'), *land, pightel* ('small enclosure'), *plott* and *teag* ('enclosure'; Sussex –tye). From combinations like Benhawe, Lynerssh, etc. is revealed the cultivation of beans, flax, barley, oats, rye, wheat, peas, pears, cobnuts and perhaps saplings ('imps'). Menecroft, Menehaghe and Menelond contain *(ge)maene* ('common') and refer to common-fields. But *croft, haga*, etc. can be found coupled also with personal-names recording private ownership; such matters of ownership we shall return to.

I have so far ignored Surrey's two most historically important *feld* names. On the border of Tandridge and Reigate Hundreds lies **Thunderfield**, 'the god Tunor's *feld*', arguably site in the ninth century of a council of King Alfred recorded at a place of that name. Which is odd, seeing as the place lies in the River Mole flats deep in the miry Weald. When we come to look at our pagan past we may unravel this riddle, and at the same time consider Reigate Hundred's former name Crichefeld (surviving in the name **Crutchfield Farm** in Horley) to which Thunderfield may be related.

Further consideration is merited also by the most interesting *wudu* name: 'the ceorls' wood'. **Charlwood** lies within sight of Thunderfield across the flatlands, or did before Horley town was built. The name presents a deliberate contrast to Kingswood and Earlswood, the latter being within the manor of the de Warennes, the Earls of Surrey at Reigate Castle. We shall return to ceorls later. Note merely that the parish name Charlwood perhaps encapsulates the social history of this part of the world since it must signify the management by 'churls' of the local resources, the 'wood'. The wood is the common grazing land abutting the once great *leah* of Horley Common; it survived to be recorded by the First Edition of the Ordnance Survey as small relict commons scattered among fields.

The geese on the common

The proximity of **Gatwick Airport** suggests what ceorls might have been grazing on their commons. Mostly place-names don't tell us, because commons, like farms, were mixed economies and their names, as we have seen, of the type Farleigh ('bracken-covered') or Norley ('north'). Exceptions are Kinnersley, with its whiff of cattle-herders, **Chaldon**, 'calves' down', and **Horsley**, to do with horses. Chaldon as an estate name is seventh century or earlier; Horsley, a substantial estate, no later than the ninth. Both cattle and horses suit downland, though horses, like cattle, thrive also on marsh. Horsley, Chaldon and Kinnersley hint at British traditions: the horse was the archetypal Celtic war machine (Horsham and Warnham, 'horse' and perhaps 'stallion enclosure', lie just over the Wealden Sussex border), while cattle were their currency. Again such names may hark back to earliest times: wide grazing-lands under communal authority.

Evidence of 'transhumance' (a geographer's term for moving with your animals and the seasons) are perhaps the pair of names **Winterfold Heath** on the dry sandstone plateau in Albury parish and **Somersbury**

Wood below in the clay vale of the Weald near Walliswood (a name we shall meet again). If so, the Surrey lowland version is the reverse of the Alpine. Several other 'winter' names occur.

Beasts of lesser importance remain unrecorded until late, except for the goats of Gatwick ('goat farm'), appearing at two more Surrey Gatwick's and at **Gatton** and **Gadbrook** (the relatively recent enclosure of the latter's common decried by Surrey's own rural hero William Cobbett, one of whose readers was Karl Marx). The fact that Gatton is recorded from the ninth century suggests reasonably early specialization into goat herding. Perhaps the undemanding goat was beast of choice for rough commoners, predating the de luxe grass-cutting sheep associated with medieval and subsequent land enclosures and the woollen industry of south-west Surrey. If the goats were for milk or cheese, they perhaps gave way to cows by the time of the Norman-French place-name in Cranleigh, **Vachery** (*la Vacherie*, 'dairy farm' in 1245). **Lambeth** however, shows that fat lambs have long been on the Thames meadows.

Lesser beasts get scarcely a look-in. Pigs were not (*pace* Loseley) regarded worthy place-namers, except in their sporting mode as at **Eversheds** (*eofor*, 'wild boar'). Honifeld ('honey') has been mentioned; the clusters of bee-hives traditionally generating welcome income on the heaths appear also in Ordnance Survey's one-time legend '**The Bee Garden**' identifying an earthwork on Chobham Common. In place-names we find **Emley Farm** in Thursley and **Imbhams Farm** in Haslemere referring to swarms of bees, *imbe*, perhaps hives, with Empshott over the Hants border taking such names back to Domesday. This feels to be heath-land activity on an industrial scale; corroborating evidence would be welcome. The geese seen in Victorian pastorals of Surrey cottages we have met already at **Goose Green**; they cackle too at **Gostrode** in Chiddingfold and **Goster** in Wotton (both 'goose marsh') recorded from the thirteenth century. In Chiddingfold likewise was a 'duck marsh' at **Ansteadbrook** (formerly Anderstrod). Were these puddle-duck, or wildfowl? That splendid old cock the Dorking, said to have been brought in by the Romans, inspired no place-names although Defoe reported the Dorking of his time the greatest goose and poultry market in England. By contrast the introduced rabbit, its meat and fur beloved of the Normans, had warrens at **Coneyhurst Hill** (now Pitch ['steep'] Hill in Ewhurst), and variously at Coney Burroughs, Coney Croft, Conyburrow and Cony Crook, a coney being a rabbit.

Merrow and the goodlands

Although I have rightly painted Surrey a land of extensive open grazing – wooded, grassy downland or heath – its culture at least from the Iron Age has focused on more fertile lands along its rivers, and along the strips of well-drained soils flanking the North Downs to north and south where settled a fair proportion of the Roman villas, and where today are found strings of villages.

Some whole parishes are named after their goodlands. **Send** is perhaps 'sandy (ground)', but good sand not hungry. We have seen **Merrow** to be Celtic 'marly (ground)', **Wonersh** to contain *ersc* referring to its ploughed land, and **Addiscombe** (not a parish) to preserve *camp* from Latin-derived *campus*, 'field', though this might refer to a common. But for riverside lands different words are used.

Hams and meads

In medieval times meadowland commanded a higher monetary value than tilled land because meadow hay allowed beasts to survive the winter. This general rule may have been modified in Surrey though, with its vast areas of common-land grazing.

A word said commonly to have been used of meadows is *hamm* (i.e. 'hemmed-in land'; though it might mean 'inside a bend' as in 'leg of ham'). This, presumably, because the best meadows often are enclosed in a river-bend; or as likely because wet land needed to be drained and enclosed by ditches. The creation of ditched and embanked 'hams' in the Somerset Levels is recorded for the great medieval monasteries there. In Surrey, *hamm* names **Ham** by the Thames near Kingston. Unfortunately *hamm* is not always easy to distinguish the completely different word *ham* (for which see next chapter). **Petersham** by Ham may be 'Peohtric's *hamm* ', or else 'Peohtric's home', but does have one recorded version with –*hamme* and has more certain *hamm* neighbours in Ham, **Balham** and **Clapham**. Again, two ostensibly identical Surrey parish names, **Mitcham** and **Mickleham**, mean either 'the great meadow' or 'the great estate', though Mickleham has a large field called I think The Ham in a bend of the River Mole. As we shall see in chapter 8, *hamm* seems able to embrace other types of farm enclosure, including those on the dry chalk Downs by **Merstham** (itself a name of uncertain meaning).

A more specific term for meadow was *mæd*. Surrey's most famous example is of course **Runnymede**, signing place of the *Magna Carta*.

Interestingly, its name *runinge maed*, 'counsel meadow', suggests it was already a meeting-place; perhaps unsurprising, because it commands the strategic middle Thames valley and lies between Staines and Windsor, sites whose political significance will emerge. *Wisc* (dialect 'wish') also meant some type of meadow, and appears in the names **Wisley** and **Dulwich**. This last is 'dill meadow', perhaps the College's playing-fields.

4. Cobham: Cofa's home

Leah is perhaps exceeded as a parish-naming type only by *ham* (I say perhaps, because of the *ham/hamm* problem). *Ham* makes names like **Cobham** or **Chobham** and is distinctive in usually having a personal-name as first element.

We tend to think of early individuals as unknowable. Some of them *are* known, and more could be. We already know fragments of the lives of several contemporary individuals associated with the county – Birinus, Cædwalla, Eorcenwold, Frithuwold, Wilfrid. To these I will add Cusa, Cerot, Cisi, Bass and more. Predictably, with the exception of a couple of kings, all of the above are ecclesiastics.

The illusion of unknowableness comes from the welter of lost and supposed seculars whose personal names decorate particular of our place-names. Who *were* Cofa at **Cobham**, Ebbi at **Epsom**? Personal-names in place-names are not the norm. The exceptions, apart from the religious types discussed elsewhere (see under *wielle, treow, stan, ingas, eg, burh*), occur largely in place-names that end in *ham* or *worth*. Such exceptions need explaining. The truth seems to be that the personal-names record landholders – the local minor aristocracy.

A Mercian import?

Ham is our word 'home'. It is sprinkled across north Surrey (illustrated diagrammatically in my Figure 3e), where it names many of today's villages. *Ham* used to be thought one of the first types of Anglo-Saxon place-naming: the farmsteads of early settlers. Not really. *ingas*, as we shall see, is earlier and names central places in Surrey, whereas *ham* does not. And even *ingas* is beaten to the draw by pre-Germanic

---

Opposite: **Cobham**. Once known as Getinges, an *ingas* name preserved at **Eaton Farm** in the parish. The villages of this part of north Surrey have been renamed comprehensively with '-ham'. Yet in east Surrey they are more likely to be '-stead', and in the south-east, '-field'. In central and south-west Surrey few place-names show any of these suffixes. Why?

names, also naming central places, in this case right in the heart of the north Surrey *ham* zone (compare Figures 2 and 3e.).

So why so many *ham* names, why so regularly distributed, and why as parish names but not central place names? These questions seem not to have been asked. Richard Coates gives us a clue when he notes that the *ham* villages **Ockham**, **Effingham**, **Bookham**, **Fetcham**, **Mickleham** (maybe), **Epsom** (once Ebbisham) and the manor of **Pachesham** hover around the Celtic-named town of Leatherhead in a *satellite* sort of way. Exactly the same could be said of the environs of the Celtic-named market town of Chertsey, where we find a list of estates attached to Chertsey Abbey in a charter of *circa* 675: **Egham**, **Chobham**, **Woodham**, **Cobham** and Huneuualdesham (old name for Oatlands). In the vicinity also are **Windlesham** and **Hersham** (if these are not *hamm* names). Together these account for most of the *ham* estate-names of Surrey apart from three poorly-defined clusters: a thinner scatter focused conceivably on the partly Celtic-named central place Croydon (**Cheam** once Cegeham), **Streatham**, **Woldingham**, **Warlingham**, **Chelsham**; a small group (**Petersham**, **Hatcham**, and **Peckham** if not *hamm)* nearer Southwark and London; and way to the south a group (**Puttenham**, **Frensham**, **Wrecclesham**, possibly **Tongham** if not *hamm)* around Farnham (itself definitely *hamm)*. To cut a long story short, it does look as if *ham* names *are* satellite to the central places Leatherhead, Chertsey and perhaps Croydon, Southwark and Farnham. Could they have been named in clean sweeps by authorities associated with these foci? Specifically, given Cobham's experience, could these be *renamings*?

We shall look at the central places in Chapter 5, but for the moment examine this concept of renaming. Might renamings occur under a new political regime? Let me suggest the new regime possibly was Mercia, the Midlands kingdom Bede records as sweeping into the London region in the 670s, and which sponsored Chertsey Abbey's charter. Seen in this light, *ham* was new place-name terminology ultimately from East Anglia; East Anglia, that most Anglo-Saxon of provinces, where *ham* central place names occur in abundance as at Swaffham, Fakenham, Saxmundham, etc.

But Surrey is different from East Anglia and its Mercian neighbour (where we find Nottingham, Oakham, etc.). In these territories, as in Northumbria, *ham* was used for monastery names (e.g. Hexham Abbey, or Medeshamstede the old name of Peterborough). Surrey's *ham* places were neither monasteries nor central places. In complete contrast to East Anglia, no Surrey market town is named '-ham'. That alone is good reason for suspecting *ham* is an import into Surrey and not native.

By decree

Effa, Fecca, Ecga, Ceabba – guess their homes.

Surrey's *ham* formula mostly involves a personal-name first-element. Elmham ('elm-tree *ham'*, the name of Norfolk's new cathedral in 673) would not be typical for Surrey. Wymondham ('Wigmund's *ham'*) or Cobham ('Cofa's *ham'*) are the standard. This is place-naming by rote, by decree.

In Surrey, these personal-names can only be those of persons who 'owned' estates when the new authority's land-clerks paid a call. The authorities labelled the estates accordingly.

Estate ownership itself was no new concept. Roman Britons were quite familiar with it, as it had powered the rise and rise of Roman villas in the late-Roman countryside, and an interesting possibility is that north Surrey's *ham* estates form part of this longer cultural history. Might these estates just be the remnants of the villa system? Not grand villas with hypocaust underfloor heating systems and subtle mosaics, but a more humble sort of villa, a natural outgrowth under conditions of Roman prosperity of the local Iron Age farmstead. Probably built of timber and a thatched roof, and subsequently disappearing under multiple re-buildings that have resulted in today's churches, manors, villages or farms on pretty much the same site.

We know that in Roman Surrey even grand villas or industrial premises could occur within a couple of miles of each other, which is much the same as the distribution of *ham* names. At Cobham there was that bath house. Some justification for the wider notion comes from the form of the *ham* names themselves. They perhaps parallel the '–ey' names of northern France (Nancy, Brie, etc.) thought to have evolved from Roman names in *–ianis* and commonly with a personal-name as first-element. These French estates *are* remnants of the villa system. Whether the same is true of the *ham* parishes of north Surrey is an open question, but one worth contemplating. After all there were several conduits bringing Roman practice into England along with Christianity during this era, namely various other papal emissaries and seconded bishops setting out from Rome and Gaul – Laurentius, Mellitus, Paulinus, Felix, Birinus, Theodore, as Bede records.

Augustine didn't go it alone; he just seems to have grabbed the limelight.

Ham scarcely made it into south Surrey, though not because the place was empty. There had been Roman villas right across the Wealden fringe at Titsey, Blechingley, Abinger, Ewhurst, Chiddingfold, Compton and probably other sites yet to be discovered. Rather, perhaps the *ham*-naming fashion never reached here. Certainly we shall find that the Mercians never reached here, which is an interesting coincidence.

The exception is that putative set of names around Farnham. They do not appear in the charter associated with Farnham minster, of slightly later date than the Chertsey one. Farnham's is a Wessex charter. Did the Wessex leadership only subsequently take up *ham,* as a sort of metropolitan fashion?

Afterwards *ham* wasn't used at all. Presumably because by that time the authorities had named all their estates. Or was *ham* simply no longer in fashion?

Worth it

Place-names containing *ham* have a parallel in those with *worth.* This is another of those awkward terms carrying a range of implications. Ekwall assesses its usual meaning to be 'homestead', arising out of earlier meanings 'enclosure', ultimately from a Germanic word for 'soil, open space in a settlement'. With the exception of the difficult but interesting name **Walworth** by Southwark ('Britons' *worth*'), most Surrey *worth* names, as with *ham,* have a personal-name attached.

There simplicity ends, because *worth* on the one hand names **Betchworth** and **Abinger**, two Wealden parishes having in their history a Roman villa and a medieval castle; this same combination occurs in **Blechingley,** which like Abinger contains the apparently significant element –*inga*- ('people'; see Chapter 10). All three parish names are equally unusual for the Weald in containing a personal-name. A moment of kite-flying: are there hints here of a longevity of locally-based feudalism? On the other hand, *worth* equally names minor manors and farmsteads across the county, such as **Tadworth, Tolworth, Winkworth,** and Pappeworth now **Papercourt.**

Ham and *worth* are what are known as 'habitative' terms, that is they refer directly to estates or settlements of one size or another, as does *tun* (see Chapter 13). By contrast, relatively few 'non-habitative' (or 'landscape') place-name suffixes are found with personal-names as first elements. A surprising partial exception is *ford*, where personal-names are said to occur at Tilford and Flanchford amongst others. Are we to gather these represent owners making causeways (see Chapter 6) on their own lands; or have such names been misinterpreted? Other instances of personal-names associated with 'landscape' place-names include **Pudmore, Binscombe, Dunsfold, Duxhurst, Petridgewood, Selsdon** and **Woodmansterne**. On misinterpretation note for Woodmansterne; Ekwall prefers *wudu gemaeres thorn*, 'thorn-bush by the boundary of the wood', to *Place-Names* 'Wudumaer's thorn', and it does sound better. *Leah* has a proportion of supposed personal-name occurrences, apart from Blechingley: **Chatley Heath, Frimley** and perhaps **Witley** and **Ockley**.

Can one take such names at face value, as examples of Anglo-Saxon private ownership of slices of the landscape? 'Private' could not normally exclude communality, as seen in *leah* and *wudu* names like Chatley Heath, Petridgewood Common and Earlswood Common where clearly the landlord has not removed commoners' rights. Supposed personal-names collect in the Godalming area, in the Weald south of Reigate, and on the fringes of Windsor Forest. These could be representative of zones and periods of colonization and the growing private ownership of parcels of land, perhaps from late Anglo-Saxon times. A striking case occurs in the pair of names, the parish **Addington** ('Aeddi's *tun* ') on the edge of the Downs and a couple of miles away on the London clay **Addiscombe** ('Aeddi's *camp*, or field'); it is assumed the same person is referred to. (A thane Addi appears in Bede for the seventh century, but we know not the date of this Surrey man).

There is evidence of private ownership for *hyth* ('harbour' see chapter 6), though that is not so surprising. But the suffixes *-eg* ('island '), *-wielle* ('spring') and *-treow* ('tree') are special cases, as will be revealed.

Farms and families

I do not cover farm names in this book as there are too many of them and most are relatively late. A good study of the early farming patterns of Surrey has been made by John Blair (1991). He suggests that small mixed farms and their associated enclosures may have been the basic building-block of rural settlement, some perhaps surviving pretty much intact from the Iron Age to the present. Others disappeared in a shift to nucleated villages with the village street and collectively-managed 'common fields' of the more centralized medieval manors.

Two of the manifestations of the long life of ancient farmsteads are the archaeological remains of 'Celtic fields' on the Surrey Downs, and certain naming practices including *hamm* for enclosed fields and *worth* for a central farmstead. Blair backs this up with reference to a Merstham boundary charter of 947 which refers to 'hamms' on the sites of modern Netherne and Woodplace Farms, and to *tunles weoth* at today's **Tollsworth Farm**. At Tollsworth the farm buildings themselves have moved; an earlier site is marked by an earthwork nearby. Either in 947 or before, this earthwork was a farm run by someone called Tunel, while equivalent *worth* terminology is taken back to the late seventh century by the Chertsey Abbey charter's reference to **Tadworth** not far away in Banstead, presumably owned by one Theodda. **Netherne**, by the way, a name recurring in Alfold, is hazarded by *Place-Names* rather coyly as '*nied-aern*, 'domus neccesaria' ', which I take to mean 'toilet'; on the other hand Clark Hall gives for *nied* various options including 'duty, compulsion' so a number of scenarios are possible.

Just occasionally a modern farm will be the sole carrier of an estate name from the seventh century: examples being **Crutchfield, Sherbourne, Binton, Eaton, Tyting** and **Tillingdown Farms**. Presumably because either they mark a redundant central place site, or because they were a detached or remote part of an estate and were named from it in the past.

Local surnames also are beyond my scope except on occasions where a family has taken the name of their ancestral holding. Evershed and Risbridger we have noted.

5. Croydon and the towns

So far we have been in the countryside. Now for the town. Can place-names tell us something about the origins of Surrey's towns? Might, for example, place-names throw light on the existence of 'missing' Romano-British central places? Might place-names relate the one age to the other? I am hopeful on both counts.

First, a bit more geography. Underpinning our towns is a wider geographical structure. For 'town' read *market-place*. And to have a market you have to have an area from which local produce is drawn.

Archaeologists say that in Roman times we could have expected to find a 'small town' every six miles or so: three miles being the distance a farmer might reasonably make it to market and back in a day. This does not seem to work for Surrey with its relatively poor soils and thus traditionally poor economy. However this may simply reflect our current archaeological ignorance. Roman suburbs or 'small towns' are known at Southwark on London's Dover road, Staines on the road to Silchester, and Ewell on Stane Street ('stone street') to Chichester. On archaeological evidence other 'roadside stations' are suspected on Stane Street at Merton/Morden at the Wandle, and Dorking near the Mole crossing, and on other roads at Bagshot, Farnham and Croydon. There is a strong likelihood that small towns existed at Burpham by Guildford, long since lost to gravel digging, and on the flats by Kingston at Waleport (see below), which met a similar fate. Until recently, these last two have been made little of by archaeologists – perhaps because they don't to fit into the accepted pattern of Roman roads, but this is a pattern we clearly need to know more about. For example, there is growing suspicion that the A3 London-to-Kingston-to-Burpham route was a Roman road, ultimately to Winchester; in which case an intermediate settlement around Cobham at the Mole crossing is probable. Potentially then, there were eleven 'urban' sites.

Which is not so different from the list of fourteen medieval market towns located on Figure 1: Southwark, Staines, Chertsey, Leatherhead, Dorking, Woking (brief life only), Farnham, Croydon, Guildford, Kingston, Godalming, Reigate, Blechingley (since failed) and Haslemere. Given that the population of mid-period Roman Britain was probably as large as in mid-medieval times, the shorter list of Romano-British centres may indeed reflect our ignorance. Alternatively, distant communication by road was easier in Roman times, so market-places could be further apart. Or was the Imperial militarized, hierarchical and monetary economy less dependent on market sites and more focused on major towns, and during the late Empire on the economies of large rural villas? Certainly, in both classical and medieval times the market pull of London was strong, and weakened the independence of town life in Surrey.

New towns for old

Some towns are newer than others. Not necessarily really new, like the railway towns that are modern **Redhill** or **Woking** (though the names are old), or a twentieth-century suburb like Sutton or Wimbledon, or even the seventeenth-century spa of Epsom. But medieval 'new towns', laid out afresh by astute feudal lords eager to catch a piece of the booming agricultural market of their day. Such fellows picked any old place-name that happened to be lying around.

Thus the de Clare's picked '**Blechingley**' when they could have called it Chivington. The de Warenne's picked '**Reigate**' when before that it seems to have been Crichefeld (though I do have an alternative theory about Crichefeld). The Bishop of Salisbury chose '**Haslemere**' ('hazel pool', apparently related to a more ancient name Haselhurst, formerly Haselora; on *ora* see Chapter 8) when he probably meant Pepperhams. Oh well, they weren't to know. As with later versions of the 'new town' phenomenon, the choice of town name is arbitrary.

But not *all* town names are arbitrary. If you can wait until the next chapter we shall explore *ford* names; here belongs **Guildford**, but also surprisingly **Leatherhead** and Kingston (at least, in the guise of their earlier names *leto ritu* and Moreford). The most obvious regularity in Surrey town names is the ending *ingas*, as at Godalming, Dorking and Woking. I shall deal with this in Chapter 10 in the context of the earliest 'Anglo-Saxon' era. No, here we have to talk about a third regularity.

Pre-Germanic central place names

Rob Poulton has said that the distribution of *pre-Germanic* place-name elements, that is names with residual Latin or Celtic bits, is 'random'. Yet it is not random. Relic pre-Germanic language haunts the sites that were to become the *towns* of much of Surrey. (Another important co-relation of pre-Germanic linguistic survival – that of significant pagan centres – will be dealt with in Chapter 8).

Look at the evidence, shown diagrammatically in Figure 2. Leatherhead's name is Celtic. True, Leatherhead was not always the focus of what became Copthorne Hundred; in Roman times that fell to Ewell. Ewell, on the edge of the North Downs where crossed by Stane Street, with its sacred pools at the source of the **River Hogsmill** (an unfortunate and not its original name, which seems instead to have been Lortbourne, 'dirty river'). To a geographer though, the place with the money is Leatherhead, where the Mole valley emerges from the Downs onto the fertile Downs-edge strip. And so it proved, once Stane Street had been re-routed (for which see Chapter 6); Leatherhead took its true place as one of the Surrey market towns. But why its Celtic name? Does this imply the place was important *before* Stane Street? Certainly it was important after; two early Anglo-Saxon cemeteries have been found there, among the most westerly in the county. (*The* most westerly is at Guildown by Guildford, which raises again the issue of the A3).

Leatherhead, in *circa* 880 was recorded as Leodridan (a name which *The Place-Names of Surrey* gave up on but thought might be garbled Celtic, while Ekwall interpreted it as Germanic *leode rida* 'the public ford') was in 1980 re-evaluated in a brilliant article, 'Methodological reflections on Leatherhead', by Richard Coates of the University of Sussex, as Celtic *leto ritu* 'grey (well, perhaps chalky-white) ford'. Instantly, Leatherhead jumped back in time by a few centuries, from being English to being Romano-British. Thus are academic revolutions made.

But Leatherhead is part of a pattern. There are Celtic names associated with virtually every medieval market town in north Surrey. This would be surprising – the official view is that no Surrey town is older than late Anglo-Saxon – were it not for Everitt's study on Kent. Alan Everitt showed that Roman central places survived in Kent to become medieval market towns, often *retaining elements of their Romano-British names*. Think Canterbury (capital of the Roman province of Cantium), Dover, Rochester, Lyminge, Faversham, Dartford. And so it seems for Surrey: at **Leatherhead, Chertsey, Croydon,** Waleport (a lost field-name in Kingston upon Thames), **Dorking** and of course **London**.

Chertsey's name has a Celtic personal-name as its first element. We can explore the probable ecclesial implications of this in Chapter 11.

Croydon's name has as its first element Celtic-derived *croh*, 'saffron'. I have a theory as to why.

Among the field-names of **Kingston upon Thames** Joan Wakeford found the name Waleport. This would seem to be *weala port*, 'Britons' port', the second element being Latin-derived and presumably meaning 'town' (or conceivably 'port').

Dorking, already suspected of being a Roman station on Stane Street, carries in its name something surmised to have been a Celtic district-name, 'Dorce'.

The point is that the names of most medieval market towns of the northern half of the county, plus the name **London** itself, are redolent with pre-Germanic undertones. This wasn't supposed to be. We shall look later at the history of the City of London, to find out why it *might* be. Note here though, in order to be a bit rigorous with the data, that some Romano-British central places seem to have survived into today's urban structure while *not* retaining any pre-Germanic place-name element. This applies at each of **Southwark** (ignoring Walworth), **Kingston** (ignoring Waleport) and **Staines**. We shall find however, that where a Roman central place has survived, but its name not, then there are understandable political reasons for the new name.

Urban morphology

First another bit of technical jargon. Urban morphology means 'the shape of towns', but geographers include the history of how towns shuffle about on their seats and have a disconcerting habit of wandering off. Any self-respecting strategic river-crossing has had at least a couple of sites, sometimes more, on the left-bank or the right, up-hill a bit or down, where give-away traces of occupation can be found. This has played havoc with our concept of how old our towns actually are.

Croydon. Long an established central place. Its name comprises Celtic *croh* ('saffron'), plus English *denu* ('dene, valley'). In other words a remarkable parallel to the town of Saffron Walden on the far side of London: *weala denu*, 'Briton's valley'. At Walden, saffron-growing is known from at least Tudor times. Were priceless culinary stamens grown in chalky vales north and south of the Thames for sophisticated Roman villas, and might this have been continued at Walden by an epicurean medieval Church?

So, with respect to the urban morphology of Surrey towns, existing pronouncements have to be taken with a pinch of salt. But archaeologists do provide helpful clues. I may be completely wrong on this, but my reading is that Surrey's urban leanings are visible in the Bronze Age and steadily matured. By that time, hilltop locations close to a strategic river-crossings seem to have been in favour. At Godalming this may have been on the plateau by Charterhouse School. At Chertsey, St Anne's Hill. At Kingston, perhaps Coombe Hill, or indeed Caesar's Camp on Wimbledon Common. At Farnham, another Caesar's Camp on a not-too-distant hill. At Guildford, was it Guildown, Pewsey Down or St Catherine's Hill? (This admittedly is a dubious reading of archaeology; the various sites are of varying antiquity, and probably of variable function).

Either way, by peaceful and prosperous mid-Roman times an in-your-face site right on the riverbank was fine. Burpham by Guildford, perhaps. Or the former island in the mouth of the River Hogsmill at Kingston. But by post-Roman times it was off again up the nearest hill for most understandable reasons (see Chapter 13). By late Anglo-Saxon or medieval times, once Alfred the Great or William the Bastard had shifted the pieces around the board a bit, a medieval fair might grow up beside a ford (as at the famous fair at Shalford by the St Catherine's Hill crossing) and then later, merchants could once more safely set up shop in an expansive Market Place-*cum*-High Street right where the road approaches a spanking new river bridge.

Are place-names relevant to the obscured histories of our towns? Perhaps not much – much of it was a very long time ago, and there has been much water under the bridge since. But occasionally there may be a glimmer. The surviving names or part-names Leatherhead, Croy(don), Cherts(ey), Waleport, Wal(worth), Dorking are all pre-Germanic in origin. And what about **Burpham** – was there a Roman *burh* here, or as likely Guildford's mid-Anglo-Saxon fortress (as known at another Burpham near Arundel)? While in the Chertsey area in the seventh-century there is recorded by the Thames a 'wealas huthe' ('Briton's harbour') to which we shall return.

So just because Roman remains haven't been dug up in the High Street doesn't mean that your town isn't as old as they come. It was probably already a gleam in the eye of our Bronze Age forebears. And though we don't have the town's Bronze Age name, we might just have its Iron Age, Romano-British or seventh-century one. In Kingston's case, *more* than one of them (see Chapter 12).

6. Tilford bridges: rivers, roads and trade

Trade existed after the Romans – albeit at a pace limited by muddy tracks, river punts and ships waiting for the tide.

In 597 King Æthelberht of Kent and his Frankish wife Bertha, a Christian, were busy with foreign affairs both religious and secular. They had a visitation from Augustine, an emissary sent from the Pope in Rome. As a result, as we shall see, the very name of **Surrey** is a creation of international influences – not local and homely at all.

Consider **Tilford**, an obscure though pleasant west Surrey spot. There are two bridges at Tilford, part of a series built across the upper Wey by the monks of Waverley Abbey to facilitate the movement of agricultural produce. In other words, *trade* – if only from farm to monastery. As an exemplar name for this chapter we could as easily have chosen **Guildford**, or **Rotherhithe**. All such names are about trade. Trade not in avocados or the latest CDs, but in luxuries nonetheless, in food, and in ideas. If volumes were low, they nonetheless were significant. Our place-names show it.

The Roman roads puzzle

The element '-ford', oddly, is no less mysterious than many others we shall come across in this book. Once in an article in the *English Place-Name Society Journal* it was suggested that *ford* names in Lancashire tended to lie on Roman roads. Margaret Gelling has denied this for Berkshire and Oxfordshire, saying there are just too many *ford* names for them all to have been on Roman roads. This however may be countered by a remark of Oliver Rackham, that most country lanes in England date probably from at least the Bronze Age. So all *ford* names could all have been on 'Roman' routes after all. Most Roman roads would have been muddy Iron Age tracks; few the perfectly engineered military artefact. Either way, it's all to do with travel; and for 'travel', read 'trade'.

I have a theory about major Roman roads. Roman roads survive today as, say, the A2 or A5 because they have continued to be useful throughout. As Rackham points out, if just one generation of our ancestors failed to clear invasive blackthorn and hawthorn from the roadbed virtually every single year (or at least tread a diversion around any new obstruction) these ancient ways would have gone the way of the trebuchet. But they didn't. Instead, they collected place-names in *ford*. They induced also names in Latin-derived *stret*, '(Roman) street', from imperial *strata*. *Stret* is rare in Surrey, though occurring on known Roman roads at **Streatham** near Croydon on the A22/23, **Stratton** and **Stansted** (*Stanstrete*, 1263) near Godstone on the A22, but also at an unexplained **Stratford** on the A3 not far from (surprise, surprise) Cobham.

My theory of *post-Roman* major roads, and it is theory only, is that where a Roman route fell out of use it was because the route, perhaps in the sixth or seventh century, was *diverted* via a newly important intermediate destination; but that such diversions commonly would have been via other, perhaps otherwise unrecognized Roman branch routes. A potential example might be the diversion of Stane Street away from Ewell and instead via Kingston upon Thames and Leatherhead: Kingston, the newly important centre of Mercia and subsequently Wessex-in-Surrey. But now *I'm* diverting, so swiftly on again.

Ford as causeway

Ford is much more frequent than *stret*. And again *ford* is not a Germanic word. It comes from the Celtic, in Welsh now *rhyd,* but in Roman-Britain *ritu* as in Anderidos, both ostensibly 'ford'. Yet Welsh *ffordd* means not 'ford' but 'road', and is said to be a loan-word from English. There *are* true Germanic words for river-crossing, though they appear but rarely in English place-names: one is *gelad* ('load') as in Lechlade, Cricklade; another, *waed* (perhaps related to 'wade') as in St Nicholas at Wade by Thanet. Yet for some reason, English mostly uses the Celtic-derived word.

In a nutshell, let us hazard that the original meaning of *ritu/ford/ffordd* was 'causeway'. In effect 'carrying-way', since the Latin cognate of *ford* is *portare* 'to carry' (whence *porta* 'gate', and *portus* 'port'). In wet Atlantic Britain most fords did not exist without an approaching causeway; without one, you wouldn't even find the ford – the two concepts are inseparable. Anyone who has been a kid in Surrey and chosen to trek across the wilder parts of its small marshy valleys will know that in the absence of a causeway one can get quickly into a very sticky situation. Most ancient causeways must lie buried under the approach ramps of modern road bridges, for example under the fine medieval stone bridges at **Tilford** and **Somerset Bridge** (*sumaeres forda* in 909) on the upper Wey.

Look at it another way. We know from archaeology that ingeniously-constructed timber causeways had been a major achievement of British engineering and social infrastructure since the Stone Age, and continued to be so into the Iron Age and indeed Anglo-Saxon eras. It would be strange indeed if there were no word for them in English place-names. True, *brycg* (our 'bridge') did once have this sense; again, this seems to have been relatively little used, though **Weybridge** and **Ricebridge** appear in this book, the former known from the seventh century. Gelling and Cole interestingly suggest that Ridware in Staffordshire, 'people of the *ritu*', may refer to a 'road through wet ground between the rivers Blithe and Trent'; this sounds like a causeway.

Either way, *ford* is an early place-name element. The *Anglo-Saxon Chronicle*, in referring to the period before 600, cites in south-east England several *ford* names. In Surrey, only in the west does *ford* generate parish names: **Shalford**, **Pyrford** and **Guildford**. The significant exception is 'Moreford', which we shall come to. *Ford* is common in west Surrey minor names too, but in east Surrey where *stret* is stronger we see of *ford* little more than **Burford Bridge** on Stane Street, then to the south of Reigate, **Flanchford**, **Cudworth** (originally Cudiford) and **Salfords**. Arguably this because west Surrey has dryish sands that suit fords, in contrast to the almost waterless chalk and the dead boggy clays of east Surrey which don't. Or could the answer yet again lie in the geography of language change?

Radial routes from of London

The three central place names **Leatherhead**, **Guildford**, and one of Kingston's lost names Moreford, and are very relevant to all this. They are part of a quite regular pattern stretching across the London Basin revealing the Roman (probably pre-Roman) bones of the regional economy, lying just beneath and still supporting 2000 and more years of vibrant economic flesh.

Look to your road atlas. See the Roman roads still reaching out across the Thames valley from London: today's A2, A23/A22, A24/A29, A30, A5, A10 and A12. On many of these hang central places named *ford*: Crayford, Dartford, Brentford, Ilford, Romford, Chelmsford. Surrey's town names are part of this.

Leatherhead's long bridge still carries a presumed ancient route along the fertile northern flank of the North Downs, over the whitey-grey chalky bed of the River Mole (though today's bridge seems to have been relocated a couple of hundred yards north from an earlier alignment). Nobody knows what the 'gold' of **Guildford** refers to, but just possibly the name relocated from the ancient river crossing of the 'Pilgrim's Way' over the River Wey by St Catherine's Hill three-quarters of a mile south of the town bridge, where the riverbed is indeed golden sand. And although Leatherhead and Guildford appear to be on east-west routes, not London radials, in fact they are on both: Leatherhead on the London-Chichester road diverted via Kingston; Guildford on a branch of the putative Winchester road. Leatherhead, *leto ritu* the 'grey-coloured *ford* ', could thus be seen as a Celtic template for subsequent 'English' *ford* names – notably Guildford, the 'yellow-coloured *ford*'.

Uncovering the post-Roman road network

The Pilgrim's Way is regarded as discredited. I am unsure why, at least in respect of its southern parallel, the version along the Lower Greensand ridge below the Downs. This east-west route is a Roman road in Kent and in the equivalent location on the other side of the Weald in Sussex. Today we call it the A25; the High Streets of Reigate and Dorking are orientated along it. The A25 is a classic 'ridgeway', at least in its sections along the Greensand ridge east of Reigate, and westwards where it becomes the A31 atop the chalk **Hog's Back** west of Guildford. The name Hog's Back is known only from William Cobbett's time, playing upon the ridgeback of ancient pig breeds.

Many routes lie unrecognized by archaeology because they were not militarily engineered. Yet the seventh-century Chertsey Abbey boundary charters reveal a landscape containing Waigebrugge (**Weybridge**) and Woburne brugge (**Woburn**), a couple of instances of 'the (old) *herestraet* ' ('army road'), Harpsford (*herepaeth ford*, on the London-Silchester road but now drowned under Virginia Water), 'a road that goes to Winchester', and 'the ridge-street' on what we now know as **Chobham Ridges**. No untracked waste this; and engineered roads (*herestraet* or *herepaeth*) broadly distinguished from the majority of lesser routes that nonetheless existed, and still exist. A geographer for example, might be attracted to the 'nodes' formed by the river crossings at Weybridge, Chertsey and Staines, and from them postulate Roman route alignments out towards Burpham via **Dunford Bridge** and **Mayford** (our A320), and Farnham/Winchester via **Broadford** at Chobham. *Ford* is potentially an analytical tool.

For my own home area in the eastern Weald, take the case of **Salfords** on the A23, 'Salfordebrugg' in 1316, and the possibility that the

Brighton Road may have a hidden history. This territory must have had at least one Roman road because the largest tile works yet known from Roman Britain has recently been discovered at Reigate. There is anyway **Worsted Green** in Merstham ('Woodstreet' in 1522). The geographer might also note the spatial intervals between north-south Roman routes leading from London past Limpsfield (a route apparently closed by the founding of the current Kentish boundary), Godstone (the A22) and Dorking (the A24), and postulate a missing parallel somewhat along the A23 alignment through Redhill or Reigate. If such a road existed, the Vale of Holmesdale with in addition its east-west route becomes pretty focal. Which may explain why the Norman Earls of Surrey built their Surrey HQ at Reigate Castle, and nearby the rival de Clares another one at Blechingley by the A22.

In the Chiddingfold area, not as remote as people make out, there was a very early medieval glass-making industry (conceivably a survival from Roman times), a Roman villa, and various local names in 'street' (**Highstreet Green**, **Ryestreet Common**, and Fisherstreet beyond the Sussex border). A nice line might extend through here from Chichester to Burpham. But I digress.

Roads and markets

Along the post-Roman roads of Surrey, metalled or muddy, rolled and plodded the trade of the times. Our parish names **Banstead** ('bean place'), **Chipstead** ('market place'), **Gatton** ('goat farm'), **Horsley** ('horse common') and especially **Rotherhithe** ('cattle port', see below) seem to tell us so. They refer to cash crops, necessarily traded. Just how far they were traded is a moot point, but traded they were, and these place-names make no sense unless one presupposes an underlying and functioning route network.

The Thames trade

But we have missed out Surrey's most important trade route, the Thames. We know this, because a seventh-century charter refers to 'the place where the ships tie up' somewhere by London or Southwark. And then we have the evidence of the *hyth* names.

Gelling has said, probably rightly, that *hyth* ('hithe') is a term indicating a regionally important harbour. *Hyth* clusters along the Thames, at Puttenhuth (**Putney**), Lambhyth (**Lambeth**) and **Rotherhithe** on the Surrey Side, Queenhithe within the City itself, and Stybbanhyth (Stepney), Erith and Greenhithe downstream. That's a lot of harbours.

We don't know how old these names are, but can guess because of three seventh-century names recorded in the Chertsey Abbey charters for way upstream: Hythe, Glenthuthe (Glanty) and *Wealas huthe* ('Briton's *hyth*'), on the bank opposite Staines. It is reasonable to conclude that river trade was at least seventh-century (well in reality, Stone Age, and certainly British).

Some of these harbours seem to have got into private hands: Putta's at Putney (recorded from Domesday), Stybba's at Stepney (known from *circa* 1000 AD). The goods in question clearly included cattle (*hryther;* Rotherhithe), lambs (Lambeth), chalk for liming (Chelsea) and gravel (*ear*; Erith). But probably also gold, beans, corn, timber, perhaps salted goat hindquarters, and a lot else beside. Trade is unlikely to have stopped when the legions left.

7. The London connection

And now a favourite subject of mine: post-Roman London.

The Thames Basin's Roman roads, shown on Figure 3a, and of course the River Thames, focus movement towards the site of London. Without London, the region's economy would be like an American doughnut – nothing in the middle. In which case one of the greatest Roman trading cities north of the Alps simply disappeared in the fifth century, to be revived in 604 when Pope Gregory directed his emissary Augustine to place a metropolitan cathedral in London. So, 'London' was reinvented by Pope Gregory? Within the same Roman walls, and still bearing its Romano-British name, Londinium? This is possible. Just not very likely.

When considering the survival or otherwise of Roman London we are dealing with probabilities, but these probabilities may be illuminated by place-name evidence.

Look to the names

There is the evidence of the *wealh* ('Briton') names. Walbrook, by Mansion House in the heart of the City, seems to mean either 'Briton's harbour' or 'Briton's (boundary) stream'. Just south of the Roman London Bridge, which may or may not have collapsed, is **Walworth**: 'Briton's enclosure'. Are these names, probably seventh-century, referring simply to archaeology – or to contemporary facts of economic and political life?

Other telling place-names within the City, nestling close to the suspected retained Roman fortification at Aldermanbury ('*ealdormann*'s fort' – itself suggestive) are Basinghall and Staining (earlier *Staining-halh*). These are *halh* ('corner') names thought to cross-reference to Basing in Hants and to Staines. Why? Were Basing, the forerunner of Basingstoke, and Staines the main *colonies* at the limits of London's purlieu, and as such did their representatives maintain bases within the City?

Collapse of Empire

The Roman Empire in Europe is known to have disintegrated into *mini-*

states based on the cities, but for some reason Britain is supposed to have been an exception. Yet it is no exception.

Aethelberht in 600 ran in effect the city-state of Canterbury – a state called Kent after its Roman provincial name Cantium. 'Andredesleage' (recorded 477) implies a Sussex city-state based on the massive Roman fortifications at Pevensey, prior to the siege and massacre at 'Andredescester' at the hands of the Saxons in 491. Similar was Eboracum (York), centre of the city-state of Deira, subsequently combined with Bernicia to form Northumbria; one or both of these provinces' names are Celtic. Roman Lindum colonia (Lincoln) became the focus of Lindsey, the latter name derived from the former and both Celtic; it was later absorbed into Mercia. There's more. The *Anglo-Saxon Chronicle* tells of the conquest of the hill-fortress of Old Sarum in 552; it survived to become a Norman city and, now re-located, names our Salisbury. And recorded for 577 was the defeat of three British 'kings' when the three 'cities' – assuredly city-states – Cirencester, Gloucester and Bath were overrun.

This incremental political take-over by the Germanic leaders of former mercenary communities can be seen to be the main gist of the pointedly-entitled *Anglo-Saxon Chronicle*'s early records. An equivalent process had already occurred across the breadth of the late western Roman Empire, with its history of Germanic emperors arising through the imperial army and attempting to set up mini-empires, until only the eastern Empire focused on Byzantium (Constantinople) survived in more or less its original form. But meanwhile every one of the British provincial capitals cited above seems to have transformed seamlessly into a post-Roman mini-state. Most retain to this day parts of their Romano-British names, almost certainly implying cultural continuity. Only afterwards did they become Anglo-Saxon kingdoms or parts of same. Then dioceses. Eventually, English county towns.

We must therefore take with a pinch of salt the over-blown rhetoric of the British ecclesiastic Gildas who writes of the violent destruction by Anglo-Saxons, apparently in the 440s, of British urban life. The only instances the *Chronicle* records of mass slaughter at cities are the siege of Andredescester, and the battle of Chester in 605, both later than the calamities described by Gildas. And even these places seem pretty quickly to have been reoccupied by somebody (Chester as once again a provincial capital; Pevensey, given its –eg name, probably as a monastery).

The City transmogrifies, again

The *Chronicle* records no fall of London. We can be sure it would have done, had a fall occurred. What the *Chronicle* does do is record the *existence* of London in 457, when, after a defeat at Crayford, 'the Britons then abandoned Kent and fled in great terror to the stronghold of London'. The stronghold? More like a collapsing city-state, with its frontier at Crayford. The *Chronicle*, commissioned as it was by ninth-century kings of Wessex, is otherwise remarkably coy about London. Not, I suggest, because London didn't exist, and hadn't controlled the Continental trade throughout; but because Wessex saw the ancient city-state as a rival. After all, when the *Chronicle* was being written London *was* a rival. It was temporary capital of the invading Danes. Before that, it had been Mercia's capital. The *Chronicle* is virtually silent about its undoubted contemporary, and by extension would have been discrete with the place's earlier status. Here was no meagre challenge to the authority of Wessex. Scandinavians similar to the Danes at London founded Dublin as a trading city; in London they (or their cousins under the eleventh-century over-kingship of Danish King Cnut) named the political 'hustings' of the City, and built important churches like St Magnus the Martyr by London Bridge. But no one talks up their political rivals.

Bede, writing from the perspective of a Northumbrian of the 730s, had need of no such reticence. One of his chief sources was Nothelm, 'a priest of the church of London'. For Bede, London was 'a trading centre for many nations who visit it by land and sea'. He describes those unfortunates who ejected Mellitus as their bishop in the 610s as London's 'people' (or 'citizens', depending on your translation).

In the dark earth

One could go on about major pieces missing from our received national history. About a reinterpretation of the late-Roman 'black' or 'dark earth' layer found in the City and at Southwark and Staines. 'Dark earth' until now has been regarded as evidence of a decline into rurality, but as Macphail and Scaife point out is better interpreted as an *urban* archaeological deposit: one of sub-Roman low-tech mud walls, thatched roofs, animal dung, fireplace-blackened earth floors and kitchen waste.

Then there is the underlying urban morphology of Watling Street. This City street, the main Roman road leading to London's companion city Verulamium (i.e. St. Albans, Bede's 'Uaeclingacaestir' or 'Watling *ceaster*'), is in the City truncated by the precinct of St Paul's cathedral. This severance probably was imposed in 604, but the diverted street may have remained the main one of the sub-Roman City for on it lies St Mary Aldermary ('Old St Mary's'), mother church to today's chief City church of St Mary le Bow. St Mary le Bow itself lies on the *later* main street, Cheapside ('market street'), of King Alfred's rebuilt Wessex capital, and leads to the revealingly named Newgate. By contrast the lost gates of the diminutive British city must have been at Ludgate and Walbrook; from these two points radiate outwards St Bride Street and Fleet Street to the west, and Threadneedle Street, Cornhill and Lombard Street to the east in archetypal 'crow's feet' patterns.

Walbrook, if 'Britons' stream', suggests either that non-Londoners subsequently settled within the City east of Bank, as well as at the now well-researched early Germanic port settlement at Aldwych ('old port') to the west, or that the Walbrook was the Londoner's port in contradistinction to the foreigners' port at Aldwych.

Within the Roman walls, the dedications of St Bride's, St Martin's le Grand and St Helen's Bishopsgate churches appear likely to be late- or sub-Roman. These possibly surviving churches parallel the suggested survival of Roman Christianity at Canterbury and its known survival in the shrines of St Hippolytus (at Ippollitts in Hertfordshire) and of St Alban (at, yes, St Albans). Bede records that Saint Germanus of Auxerre twice visited Britain, in 429 and again in the 430s, called at the shrine of St Alban and assisted in a famous victory against the Anglo-Saxons. Probably Germanus embarked through London.

In sum, we are faced with a sub-Roman city woefully shrunken from its Imperial magnificence, with the industrialised manufacture of bricks and tiles, the long-distance transport of building-stone, the stimulus of rich villas and the juicy military and civic contracts long having ceased.

City limits

Historian Sir Frank Stenton has left us a conundrum: a medieval lawsuit in which it was claimed, unchallenged, that Londoners from time immemorial had enjoyed hunting rights over all the country from the Chilterns to the Weald. Which sounds like a fair description of a city state's territory.

The possible significance of the City names Basinghall and Staining has been cited. **Staines** of the Dark Earth, a surviving Roman small town once called in Latin Pontibus (i.e. 'the bridges'), doubtless lost its Roman bridges and was by late Anglo-Saxon times known as Stana, 'the stone'. This can only refer to the London Stone that survived here into medieval times, marking the upstream limit of the City's control of the Thames, perhaps companion to the 'Britons' harbour' on the Surrey bank opposite. Companion too, of the more famous London Stone in the City, and another marked by the Ordnance Survey on the Kent bank of the Thames estuary at the other extremity of the City's influence; the age of neither is known.

Hypothesis: up until the mid-sixth century, all Surrey formed part of the British city-state of London, and was good hunting.

Saxon Surrey

A further conundrum has been set more recently by John Hines. In effect he poses the question of why, given the occurrence of early Germanic cemeteries in north-east Surrey around Mitcham and Croydon, did Anglo-Saxon culture take so long to influence the rest of the county. In the city-state of London we have a very plausible answer.

A scenario has been ably sketched by John Morris. According to him, political power in the British city-state of London was seized in the late sixth century by the city's own Germanic mercenaries (he calls them *foederati*, 'the federates', a Roman army term). The most famous of these was Ceawlin who defeated, temporarily, rival Aethelberht at Wibbandun (traditionally thought to be **Wimbledon**). Another Anglo-Saxon, Cuthwulf, took Cirencester, Gloucester and Bath. Ceawlin was over-king of southern England and London, and one of the first Anglo-Saxon kings of 'Wessex'. (Traditionally Cerdic was first, whose name and provenance John Morris interprets as British).

The *Chronicle's* 'Men of Surrey', a team who fought bravely in the ninth-century, can be slotted into this picture. They were perhaps the descendants of Hines' early Germanic communities: communities, in Morris' terms, originally *invited* to settle in strategic locations south of the capital, guarding, in exchange for land, the routes into the Weald with its strategic iron, timber and cattle supplies. Invited in by the sub-Roman British authorities, one of whose names has come down to us from the documents collected by the Briton Nennius as Vortigern, a 'proud tyrant'. The man who made the silly mistake of inviting in Hengist and Horsa, fresh Germans from the Continent.

These bold mercenaries did not invent **Surrey**, the 'southern district'. That name came only later, as we shall see. Nor were they part of some 'Middle Saxons', jointly with the county of Middlesex north of the Thames. The name 'Middlesex' seems to have been invented by Mercians to glorify, and perhaps placate, territories captured in the Thames valley when Mercia adopted London as its new capital in the late seventh century. No mythological line of kings is associated with this Middle Saxony; instead the area name is a strict parallel with that other fiction, Middle Anglia, carved at a similar time from minor British states to the west of East Anglia. But Middlessex as a fiction was one the kings of Wessex were happy enough to perpetuate, when eventually they regained Surrey and London as their own in later centuries.

Suburbs in rure

London was never again a political power in its own right, but remained an economic powerhouse and cultural fount. It was London's cultural influence that most often dominated Surrey during its various periods of seventh-century renamings. It is a fair bet that London cultural fashion mediated the choice of our *ham* parish names, and prior to that maintained our pre-Germanic central place names. We shall catch the same influence when we come to look at names containing *dun*, *stede* or *tun*.

Surrey has always been a suburb of London. Southwark certainly was a suburb from the first, a Roman one, and its nickname **The Borough** (i.e. *burh*) either means 'suburb' or else refers to the lost fortress of Suthringa Geweorche (see Chapter 8). From Southwark roads radiated out across Roman London's southern territories. Surrey as suburb of London: this is perhaps the single most important fact about Surrey place-names. It's implications have yet to be fully understood, but this role is supported, by among other things, the survival of rare Celto-Latin technical terms close to London: *port* at Waleport, *camp* at **Addiscombe**, and indeed the *wealh*, 'Welsh(-speakers)' at Waleport, **Walworth**, **Walton on Thames** and **Wallington** (to which we return in Chapter 13).

RELIGION AND POLITICS

8. Shere and our pagan heritage

I have mentioned paganism, and hinted that the conversion to Christianity represents far from a complete break. It is time to discuss this directly; to see what Surrey's place-names can tell us about our religiosity.

'Topographical' place-names

For the general reader of modern place-name studies Margaret Gelling and Ann Cole's *The Landscape of Place-Names* (published 2000) is the book of the moment. Their perspective is that many of our earliest place-name elements describe the *landscape*. I take a rather different stance, one more in line with another of Margaret Gelling's analyses. Gelling has suggested that the original meaning of *dun*, ostensibly 'hill', was in effect '(British) hill (settlement)', and I agree. Here is no describer of landscape *per se*, but one of an associated *economic activity* or *function*. Chapter 3 attempted an equivalent re-interpretation of a variety of elements including *leah, feld, hyrst*.

But not everything is economics; there is also landscape's *religious* significance. To the ancients of this country (or of any other), hills, pools, rivers, cliffs, springs, groves and marshes were not simply there, they meant something. They were visible manifestations of the gods. If a spring was worthy of a name, it was because it was sacred. This may be hard to swallow today with our more mundane view of life, but I will do my best to substantiate it using available place-name evidence.

Then there are Nicholas Higham's ground-breaking studies of post-Roman society where he argues that 'local cult centres' were at the heart of political organization.

It would nonetheless be perverse to claim that there are *no* purely topographical place-name elements. Clearly there are, in the names of many of England's forests, hills, valleys and streams. Indeed our *very earliest* place-name elements may be topographical: notably Celtic

St Catherine's Hill chapel by Guildford. St Catherine has adopted several ancient hill sites. Here, pagan undertones are revealed by the hill's older names **Artington** (formerly Hertindon, possibly 'hill of the people of the sacred hart') and the medieval Drakehull ('dragon hill').

terms like *cefn* ('ridge') or *afon* ('river', as in Avon). Others clearly are not, for example Latin-derived *ceaster* ('chester, Roman fortification', Welsh *caer*) and its Germanic equivalent *burh*. But I suggest that very little of Surrey's estate-naming is solely topographical. Perhaps only the likes of *denu*, 'valley' (as in **Croydon**, and the non-parishes **Marden**, **Polesden**), *strod*, 'marsh' (as in **Strood Green** but no parishes), *mor*, 'marsh' (**Morden**) or *mere*, 'lake' (**Merton**). Occasionally a dramatic natural feature justifies a name. Thus *hlith*, 'cliff', as in **Leith Hill** (not a parish) where probably the landslips on its southern face are referred to. **Hambledon**, a parish name recurring in other counties, seems to be 'maimed hill' and likely again refers to landslips or else to a distinctive terraced or flat-topped profile.

Hill-tops

Barry Cunliffe has pointed out that most of the Romano-British temples of rural Sussex are located inside Bronze Age hill-top enclosures.

In Surrey, with regard to sacred hill-tops, **St Catherine's Hill** and **St Martha's Hill**, both by Guildford, and **St Ann's Hill** by Chertsey come to mind. Each bore a medieval chapel. Such places are sometimes described as 'pilgrims' chapels', without quite explaining why pilgrims should want to go there. It would be obtuse to object to a pagan origin, and place-names back-up this assertion.

St Catherine's Hill is associated with its manorial name **Artington**, earlier Hertindon, perhaps 'the hill-top religious community of the sacred hart'. A similar name, now lost, existed in Kingston, while in Sussex we find an *ingas* name Harting. A totemic 'hart' (i.e. stag) is possible, given the parallel occurrence of 'boar' in *ingas* names at Barlings Abbey in Lincolnshire and Birling/Barling in other counties, and the excavation of a boar's-head-topped helmet recently reported in the news. Such names could refer to individuals called Heort and Baerla, but the hart reappears in monastery names at Hartlepool and Hartland. That St Catherine's Hill probably *was* pagan, or at least the stuff of legend and superstition, is indicated by its medieval name Drakehull – 'dragon hill'.

The name of **St Martha's Hill** has caused much head-scratching, and has been postulated to be a corruption of a Romano-Celtic dedication to the 'Holy Martyrs', which would make it rather ancient. A sixth-century urn has been found close to the chapel, and there was a legend of a giantess who shared her hammer with a companion on St Catherine's Hill, flinging it across to her. I like that story. St Ann and her hill we shall return to. Saints' names seem to have laid the ghosts, as it were. It is only a pity that **Devil's Punch Bowl** (where early morning mist can occasionally be seen curling upwards) and **Devil's Jumps** (three abrupt hills on Churt Common) are relatively modern names; Rocque has them on his 1765 map of the County of Surrey.

Hopefully, John Blair and Audrey Meaney's discussions (in *Anglo-Saxon Studies in Archaeology and History 8*, 1995) of the promontory sites of typical pagan temples will lead to the more considered examination of certain hill names. These surely include the repeated *ingas* types Upping-/Epping ('the up people') and Billing- and Goring (both 'people of the promontory'). *Bill* or *Gara* might refer to totemic swords, or to Bill and Gary. Yet the repetition of a possible sense 'promontory' may be significant, and Celtic precursors of such sites are suggested by the name Reculver, Celtic for 'great promontory', a Roman fort and early monastery on the Thames estuary that we shall have cause to visit when we come to consider *ingas* names.

Again, Surrey's Romano-British temples, normally alongside a major road, have been found usually to be sited on slight promontories. They represent a temporary, albeit in their time significant, phase of the longer picture just described.

Cruc and the burial mounds

The place-name element *cruc* is found at **Crooksbury Hill** by Farnham, and in Crichefeld the old name for Reigate Hundred (see Figure 2). Its origins are Celtic. A search of the 1:50,000-scale Ordnance Survey map of the Presili Hills and environs in West Wales shows that Welsh *crug* refers to burial mounds, usually on hill-tops, rather than simply 'mounds' or 'hills' as Gelling and Cole would prefer. The survival of this Celtic word in south-east England can only indicate the continuing social significance of these burial mounds. (I use an equivalent argument with respect to the survival of the Celtic- or Latin-derived words *funta, dun, ford, ceaster, port, stret, ora*).

It is uncertain whether Crooksbury refers to the enigmatic earthworks on the flank of the hill, one called Soldier's Ring. Crichefeld (*cruc feld*) seems to me likely to have referred originally to **Thunderfield** ('the god Tunor's *feld*') in Horley parish in the south of Reigate Hundred; **Crutchfield Farm** survives in the same parish, as did a now lost Wedreshulle, 'the god Woden's hill'. This last must have been a burial mound since the landscape is flat. (The earthworks known as

Thunderfield Castle may or may not be relevant here). We shall return to Crooksbury and Thunderfield shortly.

Other conceivable references to significant barrows occur at **Tooting**, which may contain 'toot' (with 'toll, tolt' Surrey dialect for a small rounded hill and a parallel to Tothill place-names usually interpreted as 'look-out hill'), plus Anglo-Saxon *beorg* ('barrow') in the parish name **Wanborough** and in the names **Burgh Heath** in Banstead, **Barrow Green** in Oxted, **Blackborough** in Reigate, and of course **Crooksbury**. Richard Coates (personal communication) has suggested **Coulsdon** might contain a Celtic term *cul*, 'bag- or belly-shaped hill'. If it does, this could refer to one of the prominent barrows in the area, and possibly reoccurs at Cooling in Kent close to Halstow ('holy place').

Holy wells

Sacred sites at pools and springs have fared if anything better than those at hill-tops or barrows – perhaps springs are easier to nip out to for a quick wish and a well-dressing. Some English sacred water sites are famous, Bath, Wells and Southwell among them, but many more are unrecognized.

In Surrey we have our sacred pools. *Aewiell* ('river source') names **Ewell** and also **Carshalton** ('cress Ewell'), both known for pools at the source of the River Hogsmill and River Wandle respectively. That at Ewell has brought forth Roman coins thrown as votive offerings. Significantly, neither *aewiell* nor *wielle* reoccur in any other parish name in the county except **Camberwell**, and here Richard Coates suggests a Latin-derived *camera*, 'chamber', conceivably associated with a sacred building at a wellhead of the type famously in medieval form at Holywell in Flintshire.

Roman Britain was hot on sacred springs and pools. Apart from the temple at Titsey beside a source of the River Eden, those at Wanborough are not far from a spring-fed pool by the tiny parish church. The temple on the dry plateau of Farley Heath seems for understandable reasons to have had an artificial pool dug beside it. This may have been standard practice: Saint Guthlac's *Life* records that he was led by a 'local man', presumably pagan, to a barrow deep in the Fens which had 'a sort of tank' beside it. We shall meet Guthlac again.

We are now in a position to return to the matter of **Shere** and the **Silent Pool**. This deep, allegedly bottomless clear, weedy, chalk-walled bowl carved out amongst the yew and box trees, is fed by unseen springs. Now it has a car park by it and when I last saw it a smelly and inappropriately sited cattle-slurry tank belonging to **Sherbourne Farm**. But the farm clearly takes its name from the pool, formerly 'Shirburn Spring'; this is *scir burna* – 'clear spring' – identical to Sherbourne Minster in Dorset, one time recorded in ecclesiastical Latin as *clara fons*, 'clear spring or fountain'. *Burna* sometimes means 'spring' but later generally meant 'stream' as in the various **Bourne** streams of Surrey, but *fons* in English place-names becomes *funta* (*viz.* Chalfont St Giles), and in Wales *ffynnon*, both utilized as 'holy well'. The religious power of Surrey's Sherbourne spring was refocused in the 'sub-minster' (John Blair's terminology), now parish church, a mile away at today's village of Shere to which the place-name 'Sher-' likewise migrated. The clue as to why, lies in yet another name **Albury**, that of the Silent Pool's present parish; we shall unravel this later. Meanwhile Surrey's sole surviving *funta* place-name is near Titsey at **Pitch Font Lane** (Pichesfunte 1402), associated with **Pitchers Wood** (Pychardesfeld, 1331). Pychard is unusual in seemingly being an Old French personal-name with no known local connection, so conceivably Pychard was priest at the Titsey spring in its dying days.

Other holy wells are difficult but not impossible to find. To none of their names (of the type 'lady well', etc.) does *The Place-Names of Surrey* give lengthy pedigrees, but that might just be lack of information. Bisley's St John the Baptist's Well you will find elsewhere in this book (see page 65). Then there is the strong spring that emerges from beneath St Catherine's Hill and issues straight into the Wey, and another flowing from **Mother Ludlam's Cave** within sight of Waverley Abbey. **Hascombe** also has a powerful spring and a parish name meaning delightfully 'the witches' valley'. Personally I always liked the pub at **Mugswell** in Chipstead, and am happy to believe it is St Margaret's Well, though *Place-Names* reports it unkindly as Mughole Street.

Groves

The Romans reported that the Celtic druids favoured sacred groves, but these seem to have vanished. If they existed in Surrey presumably they have been cut down, perhaps deliberately. Occasionally *leah* just might refer to sacred groves, notably at **Willey** (*weoh leah*, 'temple leah') and the parish church at **Thursley** ('the god Tunor's *leah*'), or the old minster site near Godalming at **Tuesley** ('the god Tiw's *leah*'). Over this distance of time it is perhaps impossible to know. There is a suggestion that one of the Romano-British temples at Wanborough may have been built around a sacred tree.

Personally I suspect **Wotton**, *wudu tun*, 'place in the wood', might be local equivalent to Bede's 'Adbaruae', i.e. *ad nemus* ('at the grove' – *nemus* is Latin for 'sacred grove') for Barrow upon Humber, or 'In-Derawuda' ('In the forest of the Deirans') for Beverley with its minster. The great Welsh monastery of Bangor-is-y-Coed, 'Bangor of the Wood' (see below), one suspects was only a step removed from a Druidic college. Wotton, its charming remote church set on a little rise between the woods of the North Downs and the woods (albeit some would then have been heaths) of Leith Hill, named Dorking's hundred, and Blair reckons it a sub-minster.

Late Anglo-Saxon laws inveighed against pagan practices at 'friths' (ostensibly groves) and enclosures. Surrey evidence is poor, though we have a parish name **Pirbright** (*pyrige fyrhth*, 'pear-tree frith'), and pears appear again at **Pyrford**, at **Parley Bridge** (where an instance of an –*inga*– form, Parlingeford, could indicate this once the meeting-place of Godley Hundred), **Perry Bridge** (one-time meeting-place of Blackheath Hundred), and **Purley** by Croydon. What's it with pears? Apples get no look-in. Did the Surrey ancients get high on bubbly perry at significant dates in the calendar? No mention of mistletoe though.

Trees, stones and pillars

Trees raise the question of sacred trees, and sacred stones. In the pagan Germanic and Scandinavian traditions, the sacred manifestations of spring, tree and hill cluster together; in Ireland, a holy well not uncommonly is o'er spread by a sacred ash tree.

The appearance of 'ash' (*aesc*) in the Surrey parish names **Ash**, **Ashtead** and perhaps in the *ingas* name **Eashing** – in a county where ash-woods are too frequent to mention, and not over-useful economically – is suspicious. On the flanks of Yscridd Fawr above Abergavenny a large ash tree dips its roots into a spring and rivulet; locally, an isolated such tree could easily stand for Yggdrasill, the World Tree of pagan Germanic tradition, or its Celtic equivalent, since it feeds so obviously on sacred waters. In other counties Ashwell (*aesc wielle*) occurs as a name for wells, suggesting that impressive ash trees sited at springs were regarded as special; whereas other trees rarely lend their names to springs. I have been fortunate to visit a partially surviving pagan site at Faha in County Clare, a churchyard with Celtic crosses, ruined chapel and two boulders, one large said to have been lifted competitively by men at weddings and the slightly smaller by the women. In the adjacent field is a natural spring with oval stone basin, small votive statuette (modern), and overhanging all a 'sacred ash' with ancient fallen branches lying around. The farmer said that on his parents' advice, and 'just in case', he never used the wood from this tree.

Most trees of course, and presumably most stones, were not sacred. Some were boundary markers, others secular meeting-places like the 'pollarded thorn' of Copthorne Hundred. But 'tree' (*treow*) sometimes meant '(Christian) cross', as in Oswestry (in Welsh, Croesoswald, 'Saint Oswald's Cross') and one suspects at the abbeys of Coventry and Daventry (respectively Cofa's and Dafa's 'tree'). In Surrey we can raise only **Tilburstow** ('Tilbeorht's tree'), now the name of a prominent hill by Godstone. Was there something on its top? **Godstone** itself seems to be 'Cod's stone', of some importance to somebody, though the antiquarian Aubrey thought it was 'God's stone' from the quality of its cut building-stone (the suffix might in fact be *tun*). **Brixton** ('Beorhtsige's stone') gave its name to a hundred. We have noted already the political significance of the Stone of **Staines**.

Pagan sacred pillars are well-known to academia. In the Celtic tradition pillars were set upon mounds. One wonders whether *caeg* ('key', and – figuratively according to Clark Hall – 'solution, explanation', but perhaps variously 'peg, post') is relevant here. It appears with *hoh* (another fascinating element, see later), *ball* (perhaps 'hill') and *hamm* ('enclosure') in other counties: Cashio/Cassiobury, Cainhoe, Keysoe, Cabus, Cainham. Could it refer to pillars, either on a mound or within a sacred enclosure? In Surrey is **Kew**, a possible *caeg hoh* name, though variously interpreted as 'quay *hoh*' or 'key-shaped mound'; though which of the pillars in the gardens today is sacred, I know not. And what of *pal*, if 'pole', seen at **Polesden Lacy** and at the Sussex *ingas* place Poling? Interesting might be also the 'pike' (if not 'peak') at the *ham* or *hamm* of **Peckham**, perhaps relating to the abrupt One Tree Hill beyond Peckham Rye Common; and come to that *bealg*, perhaps 'bulge, hill' (maybe referring to Bedford Hill by Tooting Bec Common) with *hamm* at **Balham**. More convincing is Northumbria's Shaftoe, 'shaft *hoh*', where Bobby came from.

Sacred enclosures

With respect to sacred enclosures certain *hamm* names are of particular interest. **Farnham** is 'bracken-covered *hamm* ' and might relate to some abandoned Roman enclosure since this central place, now town, founded with its church in the seventh century, lies hard by significant Roman sites. The Celtic *cader* (perhaps 'fort') of **Caterham** presumably relates to the Iron Age hill fort of **War Coppice** (whose *geweorc* is 'structure'), so is Caterham's *hamm* the fort itself? **Pepperhams**, a remote and minor central place, was in the thirteenth century relocated by the Bishop of Salisbury to become the medieval 'new town' of Haslemere; Pepperhams was the old name of Haslemere parish and the off-centre parish church is sited there still. Is its *hamm* the religious enclosure? When we come to look into the 'pipers' ostensibly referred to in this name, we may well conclude that it is. Compare Bisley church, near where a tenth century charter records an *eccles hamme*, i.e. 'church enclosure'. This is a rare example of a British term *ecles* drawn from Latin *ecclesia*; John Blair identifies the site with St John the Baptist's Well, a sacred spring at which baptisms were still being performed within recorded times.

It is easy to believe that sacred enclosures might display cultural continuity with the spectacular native enclosures of the Stone Age. Look also to the severed heads that featured in the Celtic religious and military canons; also to animal heads as totems. Much favoured were ox-heads, since dug up at some temple sites, but other animals figured too. In Surrey are **Worm's Heath** ('snake's head') in Chelsham, **Evershed** ('boar's head') in Ockley where it survived also as a surname, and **Heronshead** (actually Ernesheved, 'eagle's head') in Leigh. Such names bring to mind the various minor place-names noted by Gelling and Cole in which *healh* (one of Ekwall's definitions of *healh* being 'a retired or secret place') is combined with a wild animal or bird name. Classic pagan enclosures, I'd say.

Major cult centres

We are now perhaps in a position to assess whether Nicholas Higham's notion of 'cult centres' could explain a few things about Surrey's early past. I will look especially to two apparently obscure sites in south Surrey, **Peper Harow** and **Thunderfield**, both shown in Figure 2. I suggest that these two justify what the *hearg* of Peper Harow is *said* to designate – a 'regionally important temple'.

Peper Harow, a diminutive parish in south-west Surrey near Godalming, is either to do with someone Pipera, or is 'pipers' *hearg* '. That it might indeed be the latter is encouraged by its repetition at the Pepperhams (*pipera hamm)* we have noted as the name of Haslemere's church site, and at the *ingas* name Peppering in Sussex. Quite conceivably we hear in this odd term some distant echo of pagan ceremonial at such sites. If so, the cultural significance of this documentary relic is difficult to overestimate. The *hearg* itself has never been found. It might lie near Peper Harow church, or possibly on the promontory a mile away at **Eashing** found by archaeologists to have been ringed by the temporary ramparts of the fortress mentioned in a document called the *Burghal Hidage.* The fortress of Eashing disappears in later versions of the *Hidage* in favour of a new one at Guildford six miles away, the latter surviving in spirit at least as Guildford's royal castle though its site was perhaps as likely at **Burpham** (with the second Burpham near Arundel, a *Burghal Hidage* fort and presumably *burh hamm,* 'fort enclosure'). Another way of looking at all this is that the *centrality* of Guildford to Surrey was perhaps derived from the political influence wielded by a pagan temple at Peper Harow in the mildly fertile enclave valley of the upper Wey valley, 1,500 years ago.

And east Surrey? If Peper Harow reflects a shift of political influence in post-Roman times away from the threatened Thames towards the remoter and therefore more secure Wealden territory (or possibly simply a greater *independence* of these remote areas), is the same tendency visible in east Surrey? The answer has to be yes. At Tunor's **Thunderfield** and its environs in the rich flats of the upper Mole lies a locality stiff with suggestive nomenclature: Wedreshulle ('the god Woden's barrow') recorded in 1273, **Lowfield Heath** (*hlaw feld,* 'barrow field'), **Burstow** ('*burh* at the meeting-place' – *burh* being possibly military or monastic, and *stow* a term thought to refer to sacred meeting-places), plus the old hundred name Crichefeld if surviving as **Crutchfield Farm** (*cruc feld*). This last name presumably predates but is related to rest of the set. The final clue is **Horleyland Farm** recorded *circa* 1350 as Holyland, 'holy land'. Which brings to mind Halliford ('holy ford') in the Thames flats of west Middlesex where are similar fat grazing marshes and where religious centrality is marked by a Romano-British temple at Heathrow and an impressive and recently exhumed Stone Age avenue or 'cursus', all overlooked by the *hearg* of Harrow on the Hill. (For a significant marsh elsewhere see that of the River Till beside Yeavering – Celtic Gefrin – the British and subsequently first Anglo-Saxon centre of Bernicia in Northumbria).

Were the succulent grasses of the upper River Mole (albeit now partly under Gatwick Airport) our local equivalent, with aspirations to similar economic centrality, and governed similarly by a religious mystique of marshlands stretching back to the Stone Age? Did its political pull last up to and include the time when King Alfred trekked the half-dozen miles through sticky Wealden clay to hold a council at Thunderfield (if this is indeed the Thunderfield in question), and beyond, explaining the choice of Reigate for the site of the Norman Earl of Surrey's castle? It's just a pity we have this urge to dump airports on our most sacred places.

With these two ostensible major cult centres, Peper Harow and Thunderfield, the Surrey Weald was no backwater. If the history of King Caedwalla (whom we shall soon meet) is anything to go by, Surrey may occasionally have acted as power-broker. It was geography really: the districts centred on Peper Harow and Thunderfield enjoyed a clear 20 miles distance from any political rival, be it Rochester, Pevensey, Chichester, Winchester, Silchester or London, and might at the same time act as pivots or conduits between these differing spheres of interest (known in Anglo-Saxon times as Kent, Sussex, Wessex, London, plus subsequently an intrusive Mercia).

A model

Beneath the significance of a regionally-important temple like Peper Harow or Thunderfield, we have sites the like of **Crooksbury**. Crooksbury: a high isolated sandstone hill with a ragged fringe of pines and a Celtic name, undertones of a lost sacred barrow, and sitting next to a lost royal centre at Bintungom (now **Binton Farm** in Seale) of whose official relocation to Farnham Minster by royal charter we shall find, amazingly, we still have documentation. Crooksbury-*cum*-Bintungom-*cum*-Farnham is a fine hundred-level pagan centre within Farnham Hundred. But I have made several assumptions here.

So, a model; a three-part model, in fact.

> ✧ *Regionally-important pagan centres* occur at one or
>   more per modern county;

but below them,

> ✧ *lesser pagan centres* are to be expected at a rate of
>   one per *hundred* (see Figure 2)*;*

and beneath them,

✧ *least-important pagan centres* are to be expected in nearly every subsequent medieval Christian *parish*.

I justify this model by noting the two candidates for (sub-)regional status: **Peper Harow** and **Thunderfield**. Thereafter, candidates for centrality in a hundred include **Crooksbury** in Farnham Hundred, the **Silent Pool** in Blackheath Hundred, **Ewell**'s pools in Copthorne Hundred, the **Titsey** spring-head in a lost Limspsfield Hundred, and so on. These putative hundred-level *religious centres* seemingly are paired with *royal centres* (ie. **Seale**, **Gomshall** in Shere, **Ewell**, though any royal centre near Titsey is lost) in much the same way as can be observed in the comparable administrative unit of medieval Wales, the cantref, which normally had a royal focus paired with a monastery a couple of miles away.

Finally, the smaller pagan sites. Note how many Surrey parish names I have rendered explicable, albeit tentatively, as pagan site descriptors: **Carshalton**, **Camberwell**, **Ash**, **Pepperhams**, **Thursley**, **Kew**, etc., as well as hundred focal ones at **Shere**, **Ewell**, **Burstow**, **Seale**, **Caterham**, etc. To understand the processes involved we can do no better than visit the Welsh Marches, where the '-stow' ('sacred meeting-place') parishes of south Herefordshire and east Monmouthshire intercede between English '-church' parishes and Welsh 'llan-' ones, though the language boundary between Celtic and English has moved yet further on. The story goes that in 550 King Iddon gave land at Llantilio Crossenny to Teilo, later Bishop of Llandaff, since Teilo earlier had blessed Iddon in the latter's fight against the English. Subsequently a cross (Crossenny is 'Iddon's cross'), and then later again a church, was set up on a *pagan mound* here. I have every reason to believe that an equivalent process occurred at a **Thursley** or a **Hascombe**.

Now, this could explain The Mystery of the Missing Bodies. Pre-Christian cadavers have been elusive. We do know of Romano-British urban cemeteries outside city gates. We know sixth-century Anglo-Saxon-culture cemeteries at Croydon, Mitcham and the like, probably of the *foederati*. We know also, ostentatious late seventh-century barrows at Coulsdon, Banstead and Beddington containing the remains, as Rob Poulton has observed, of exceptionally tall men with Germanic military accoutrements; heroic burials of a type described in *Beowulf*. Probably they represent the sort of local warlord that arises in militarized societies simultaneously experiencing civil and economic collapse. In north-east Surrey such men seem likely to be the descendants of the *foederati*; in far south-west Surrey their equivalents (with different burial rites) may have been Britons. Frithuwold, Huda, but also Caedwalla perhaps are exemplars, and you may seek them in these pages; the last gasp of a social phenomenon about to be largely killed-off in a pincer movement by the Church and by the local and national over-kings of the emerging 'seven kingdoms' of late Anglo-Saxon England, known as the Heptarchy.

No, none of these are the bodies in question. Those missing from archaeology are rather the majority of post-Roman, and indeed Iron Age and rural Romano-British corpses. And country churchyards might be first place of search. Could a proportion of our churchyards have developed from earlier burial sites? Especially when the site is round, or set on a little rise as at Oxted, or at Tandridge, Merstham, Reigate, Wotton, Worplesdon, Witley, Thursley, St Martha's. Look to your own churchyard. (However, I risk over-stating the case. Romano-British and sub-Roman cemeteries have been found at a number of rural locations in Surrey, and pre-Christian cremation, as important as inhumation, leaves little trace in the absence of a barrow or urn).

A tale of two charters

Other evidence on the change from paganism to Christianity, and some associated impacts on estate naming, is provided by the two early charters Surrey is fortunate to possess. **Chertsey Abbey**'s Mercian charter dates from around 675; the Wessex charter associated with **Farnham minster** (a term I shall explain) from around 685. These precious survivals contain two estate lists and a few personal-names. Though close in date, they document contrasted social landscapes.

Chertsey's charter arose in the relatively sophisticated Thames valley. As we shall see, Christianity may have survived here from British times, and Roman agrarian techniques also may have survived; this, in spite of periodic social crises and invasion. When, as I suspect, the Mercians imposed on their north Surrey estates the East Anglia naming formula *ham*, they accurately predicted the location and names of our future parishes. Look at it the other way. When, probably in late Anglo-Saxon and early Norman times, 'parish' churches were built by the local landholder (sometimes this was Chertsey Abbey itself), they did so on estates already identified in the late seventh century.

Farnham on the other hand, lies in the Weald. There had been villas and Roman industrial activity here too, but even a decade after the Chertsey date the Farnham document mentions no *ham* places, though one possible privately-owned estate is cited, Bintungom, referring to someone Binta and identifiable with **Binton** now in Seale parish. Otherwise, it cites a pagan temple, *Cusan weoh* ('Cusa's temple'), identifiable as **Willey** ('temple *leah* ') near Farnham, and apparently a wasteland, **Churt**. Let me suggest that in reality these three were the names of *religious institutions* being subordinated by order of King Caedwalla to his new Christian minster. The first, Bintungom, I shall propose as an extant proto-minster at a royal holding at Seale (see Chapter 10); the second, clearly a pagan site, possibly an as yet un-recovered Roman roadside temple on the Winchester road west of Farnham; the third, perhaps the Roman temple now suspected on Frensham Common, with Churt in effect equivalent to another dialect *ceart* name Chard in Somerset, *ceart renn*, '(religious) house on the heath'. If so, we have a neat exemplar of my model: the hundred of Farnham is revealed to have had a principle pagan focus at Crooksbury-*cum*-Seale with subsidiary ones in what are now Farnham and Frensham parishes. Indeed, I have a suspicion (which might be wrong) that the anomaly of *ham* names way to the south of the Thames around Farnham could be removed if they were re-assessed, like Farnham, as *hamm* names, and that each (**Frensham, Puttenham, Wrecclesham, Tongham**) represents a local *pagan enclosure* supervised by the person named, rather as a pagan priest Cusa may have supervised at Willey.

Note in passing that the Weald perhaps had cast off most, but not all vestiges of Roman structure and had partially reverted to native Iron Age. Because we are here within the territory of the lost provincial capital Silchester – the one Roman city in south-east England not to survive. It was the Wild West of those days, Caedwalla's stamping ground, where more elaborate native pagan organization might still have flourished. Yet this organization, with centralities at both 'hundred' and 'parish' level, may not have been so different from the Christian system that superseded it.

The Nower, and the ancient of days

Just possibly, Wealden place-names give us a glimpse into an even more ancient past. The Latin-derived term *ora* figures strongly at the dawn of England, in the sites the *Anglo-Saxon Chronicle* claims as landing-places of the South Saxons and the men of the future Wessex, at Cymenes ora and Cerdices ora respectively, reputedly in 477 and 495. That these names refer to more than beaching-sites is hinted by the fact that *ora* seems to be Latin 'bank', and that Cerdic, although given as the name of the invading leader, is as John Morris points out

Celtic (as in effect is another so-called invader 'Port', a garbled version of the name of the Roman fortress of Portchester). The logic, I suggest, is that Germanic adventurers were allied with Cerdic, a local British king; Cerdices ora was then the name of Cerdic's ceremonial enclosure – perhaps the Iron Age hill-fort of Tatchbury near today's Ower (*ora*) and the royal *ingas* site Eling at the head of Southampton Water.

Note then the hill above Oare ('Aet Motenes oran', in 934) in the Vale of Pewsey; it has a vast Bronze Age enclosure too weakly embanked to be defensive. By the Roman promontory fort and Kentish monastery of Reculver, Gelling and Cole note an Oar Farm.

In Surrey, we have a Bronze Age enclosure by **Nore** ('at the *ora*') **Hill** at Worm's Heath (see above), while **Radnor** ('red *ora*') lies just below Holmbury hill-fort (the name being identical to Radnor in the Welsh Marches, where I believe a large prehistoric enclosure has been identified). Which does make you wonder about **The Nower** ('at the *ora*', again) by Dorking and **Nower Hill** by Headley, both once bald heathery tops (The Nower has an unexplained Bury Hill, *burh*, which might perhaps mean 'town hill'). Let alone the chalk hill of royal Windsor (one of a group of difficult *windels ora* names), site of a synod long before the Norman kings chose it for their principle residence.

My intuition is that in *ora* we have a remnant of *pre-hundredal* organization, which merited Latin terminology because the Roman administration chose to recognize its role in native political life. I have no proof.

9. Southwark, that is Surrey

I have implied already that there may be less to the name **'Surrey'** than meets the eye. It is *not* the signifier of a proud, long-lost Anglo-Saxon mini-state. My chapter title gives the game away. 'Surrey' is very closely related to the name of **Southwark**.

The Church Triumphant

In this book I emphasise the Church. The Church Triumphant was crucial for more than one reason. One, as I have said, was its being for centuries the sole literate institution (though again here are undertones of the Druids, who in Ireland wrote in ogam, a version of Latin script). That alone is enough to make the Church central to early English place-naming, or at least, name-recording.

The Church had a clear field in the matter of recording 'official' place-names, and we must not be at all surprised if it used it. Also, the Church was crucial in the regaining of social stability after the turmoil and economic collapse of the late Empire. Many of the early ecclesiastics – the 'saints' – were strong characters indeed. We meet one or two of them in these pages, including Bede's redoubtable Wilfrid and the more elusive Maelduib and Bass. These lads (sometimes, as we shall see, lasses) succeeded in getting many a rampant warrior to lay down the sword.

The bretwaldas

But the Church didn't have it all its own way, as every amateur historian knows. To understand the odd world of humans, you must have a bit of politics. (And also economics, but we've done that bit). We are not going to get far in this matter of place-names without politics, and there is necessarily quite a lot of it in this book, so here's a bit more.

Bede (and the *Anglo-Saxon Chronicle* following his example) gives a list of the over-kings of England. The *Chronicle* 's term is *bretwalda* (meaning either 'broad-wielders', 'broad kings' in the Celtic manner of the High Kings of Ireland, or 'Britannia-wielders' in a Roman sense, i.e.

Emperor of the Province of Britain). The first two *bretwalda*'s are stated to be Aelle of Sussex followed by Ceawlin of Wessex. But these are mere warlords, adventurers.

The first real over-king is Aethelberht of Kent. He too starts out adventurer, gets interrupted by Ceawlin at Wibbandun, but succeeds eventually and gains power over London. One suspects the bottomline in *bretwalda*-ship is indeed control over the prestige and international port of London. Aethelberht establishes himself in full regal manner. He and his forebears had taken over Kent as a battered but intact Romano-British going concern, didn't bother changing the Roman provincial name, and settled down in the Roman city of Durovernon as their capital. With Bertha, his Frankish Christian wife, pagan Aethelberht cultivates European ways. In 597 Pope Gregory in Rome assesses him a suitable candidate for the re-introduction of Roman ecclesiastical order into the detached province of Britain. Aethelberht changes his capital's name to Canterbury, perhaps meaning, for reasons to be explained in the next chapter, 'the cathedral of the people of Kent' and secures for it the archbishopric of southern England (though as mentioned, Gregory had envisaged London as his British metropolitan).

Saint Augustine

So, the pope sends his emissary, the man we have come to know as Saint Augustine – a tetchy fellow who later in his mission falls foul of the still-active British bishops of Wales and the West Country who, affronted by his imperiousness, give him the cold shoulder. As a unifying organizer, Saint Augustine is not a total success. But in Kent and its dependencies, and with Aethelberht's help, he makes great strides. A cathedral is founded first in Aethelberht's capital, then in 604 another at Rochester and another at London. Three Roman cities re-accredited. But Augustine achieves more than that: '**Surrey**' is down to him.

Ge equals Kentish ecclesiastical district

The name Surrey is *suther ge*, 'southern district'. But what is it 'south' of? Not Middlesex. Rather, St Paul's. To understand this, one has to understand *ge*, because here is no ordinary place-name element. For a start, it is extremely rare – only seven examples are known.

Ge, the English form of German *gau* ('district'), is almost confined to Kent. In fact to east Kent. Arranged roughly in a circle around

Canterbury are Eastry, Lyminge, Denge and Sturry. Eastry is the district to the 'east'. Lyminge is the district of the River *Limen* (the Romano-British name of the River Rother, and equivalent to the 'Limp' of Limpsfield). Denge embraces Dungeness, but is focused at its governing centre Denge by Chilham in the vale (*denu*) of the upper Stour. Sturry is the district of the lower Stour (another Celtic river name). Lyminge and Sturry follow a pattern seen already in this book: Romano-British place-names suffixed and 'explained' by an English add-on.

My own reading of this distinctive geographical patterning of Kentish *ge* is that it names *ecclesiastical districts* into which the province of Canterbury was demarcated under Augustine's influence. The whole thing is very organized and very Roman. *Ge* is simply an Anglo-Saxon translation of the relevant term in ecclesiastical Latin (probably *regio*, 'region').

Only three other *ge* names are known, all outside Kent. One is a whole county, Surrey. Another is an obscure place Vange, 'fen district', on the Essex Thames estuary, not too far from one of Bede's named monasteries, Tilbury. The last is Ely, 'district of eels', the famous cathedral of the Fens, and this last is the giveaway. An early source, *Liber Eliensis*, says that when Queen (subsequently Abbess) Etheldreda founded her abbey at Ely in 673 she deliberately adopted a site beside the ruins of a former foundation of Saint Augustine's – in effect, re-founding it. Quite likely a religious foundation of Aethelberht's empire of *circa* 600 could have become abandoned by the 670s, since Bede records that in the interim both London and Kent went through wobbly patches of renewed paganism following King Aethelberht's death in 616. But the fact that Ely was an Augustinian church suggests that the *eg* 'district' system was *a system of minster territories in the Roman manner*. Surviving *ge* names are a memory of this Augustinian system, visibly spanning Aethelberht's authority throughout Kent, London, Surrey, Essex and into East Anglia.

The first Anglo-Saxon minsters

A minster is known otherwise as a 'mother church', often the first church founded in a district and one which held an organizing position with respect to churches subsequently founded in the locality. Minster functions waned as the centuries passed but in this early period they were central, though subsidiary to one or two focal cathedrals with their bishop in each of the main kingdoms – the

Heptarchy – of Anglo-Saxon England. The origin of cathedrals and minsters is the munificence of popes in Rome, themselves harking back to the status of the Christian Emperors of the late Empire.

This model of *ge* requires that at the heart of each Kentish *ge* district stood an early Roman-style minster, which does seem to hold at least for Lyminge, Sturry and Eastry. Then, after a hiatus following the death of Aethelberht, King Egbert and his notably devout brother and successor Hlothhere (their mother became an Abbess of Ely), leading up to and following the crucial synods of Hertford and Hatfield in 673 and 680 (of which more later) set about re-establishing and restructuring the Kentish ecclesiastical system. A similar and parallel process seems to have occurred in the important kingdom of East Anglia under Sigbert and Anna, others of Bede's devout kings (Etheldreda re-founder of Ely was Anna's daughter). We shall have cause to recall further estates-*cum*-monasteries of Anna's, Exning and Blythburgh, in the next chapter.

Which is a very long-winded way of saying that 'Surrey' was in all probability a Kentish-controlled minster territorial name, rather than a county as such. And no kingdom.

Southwark and Surrey

Where was Surrey? This sounds a daft question, but what I mean is: what was the site of the Kentish minster upon which the minster district called '**Surrey**' was centred?

I suggest there is a candidate list of one. The Priory of St Mary Overy, 'Over the River Thames', **Southwark**. This became Surrey's cathedral only in 1540 and is a fine medieval building. As monastery it had had secular canons from 852, but by tradition was founded as a nunnery at the start of the seventh century. Its name, *suth (ge)weorc*, means 'southern building', and thus probably 'southern monastery', rather as **Newark Priory** in Surrey means 'new monastery'.

Surrey and Southwark are 'south'. South of London Bridge. South of the city controlled by Aethelberht, south of St Paul's. Aethelberht and Augustine planted a Kentish minster at Southwark 'south' of the cathedral of London, as Eastry is 'east' of the cathedral of Kent.

In the 670s, as already described in Chapter 4, the Mercians came to rule in London and Surrey. But in their charter for **Chertsey Abbey** they specifically cite an extant Chertsey charter of Egbert of Kent, a decade earlier. Although Bede says Chertsey Abbey was 'built' by the ecclesiast Eorcenwold, I would guess re-built or re-located, given that the abbey's name embraces a Celtic personal-name probably indicating an earlier abbot (see below). Eorcenwold is described by Bede as a devoted and influential man, latterly Bishop of London, and a signatory also of Wessex's Farnham minster charter. In their Chertsey charter the Mercians cite the name of the 'province' in which Chertsey lies: 'Surrey'.

In fact Wulfhere of Mercia's new man on the spot, Frithuwold, is described as 'sub-king of Surrey'; certainly the charter allocates to the abbey estates seemingly including everything within the two nearest hundreds (an institution I shall shortly explore) of Godley and Elmbridge, but in addition a string of estates across the middle of today's county from Chaldon to Clandon. This is a vast area, though perhaps not the whole of Surrey as we know it.

My guess is two-fold. Firstly, that the Mercians through this charter were consolidating their hold on territories newly captured south of the Thames. And secondly, following Kentish practice, they were selecting a single ecclesiastical centre to act as 'pro-cathedral' for these territories. They followed Kentish practice extremely closely, because although Kent's local minster may originally have been at Southwark, it seems likely that after the hiatus following Aethelberht's death this status was shifted to Chertsey: hence Egbert's charter of the 660s. Southwark had gone into temporary decline, the same as did Ely. But the Mercians, and doubtless Egbert before them, retained the existing Kentish name for this pro-cathedral diocese: 'Surrey'.

The contemporary Mercians were diplomats and well as invaders. King Wulfhere, Mercia's new *bretwalda* (though neither Bede nor the *Chronicle*, both enemies of Mercia, admit to this) was laying overtly the foundations of a future national kingdom that would replace Kent's more limited superiority but replicate that of Edwin of Northumbria (for whom see below). A re-united Roman Britain. The most famous Mercian over-king was to be Offa in the next century; the one who organised Offa's Dyke along the frontier with Wales. You see, it's all politics. Oh, and religion.

So was Surrey born.

10. Dorking and the Hundreds

First, there was geography.

Surrey's main river names are Celtic, the **Thames** and the **Wey**. The **Mole** was the Emlyn, renamed as mentioned from its exit into the Thames at **Molesey** (as the **Wandle** was renamed after **Wandsworth**); 'Emlyn' survived into the eighteenth century. Such names connect Surrey's rivers with the wider Celtic and Indo-European world, where they are replicated in the Wye, Medway, Teme, Tamar and the extremely distant Tamasa a tributary of the Ganges. No one knows what Emlyn means, though Ekwall notes it is the same as Emen, the old name of the Nar in East Anglia. Probably the name Mole suits it as well, what with the famous swallowholes below the box-shrub-clothed slopes of **Box Hill**, where in dry weather 'the river runneth under' to re-emerge at Leatherhead Bridge. I have been lucky enough to see that once; to walk in the dry chalky bed of the lost Emlyn.

The hundreds

Geographers will tell you that river basins generate market towns. If these basins are longer than half a dozen miles, more than one town may be born, each with its own territory. Such divisions of the landscape started life town-less, as virtually self-sufficient economic regions blooming with the first Neolithic (New Stone Age) farmers. Later, they were called the hundreds.

Hundreds sometimes point to 'failed' towns. Shere in Blackheath Hundred, Woking in Woking Hundred, Blechingley in Tandridge Hundred, all had rather brief lives as market places (though Woking is making up for lost time). I will suggest 'lost' hundreds on the basis of suspected central place names: notably **Tooting** and **Limpsfield**, that seem unconnected with subsequent hundred boundaries. **Elmbridge** Hundred is an instance of being spoilt for choice. The name is 'bridge over the Emlyn'; but was the bridge in question that at Molesey, Esher or perhaps Cobham? Is one of these a lost central place? (For a possible answer, that of 'all three', read on).

The string of Surrey towns along the fertile southern edge of the North Downs (Bletchingley, Reigate, Dorking, Guildford, Godalming,

Farnham), facing the Weald, are firmly settled on their sites by virtue of occupying entrances to river-gaps through the Downs. These gaps, some of them long dry, might be thought to have offered the best routes to drag a wagon up and over to the Thames valley. But a little incline meant nothing to Roman road-builders, and a more important rationale might be the decent valley routes for the droving of cattle. The routes still exist today, labelled the A22, A23, A24, A3 and A31, though the Romans doubtless called them something different. The principle advantage of these towns sites probably were the damp flatlands the rivers penned up against the Downs (see Figure 1): **Nutfield Marsh** between Blechingley and Reigate, the Brockham flats by Dorking, **Peasmarsh** lying between Guildford and Godalming, and the Blackwater and Wey meadows around Farnham. These grassy pampas must have offered perfect collecting grounds for Wealden cattle being driven north. In effect, Surrey's town sites, at least as general localities, were marked out well before the Iron Age; they just took a long time to grow. You want proof? Look to Riverhead by Sevenoaks, in an equivalent zone just over in Kent. Riverhead is *hryther hyth*, 'cattle shipping-place', and next to it another **Chipstead** ('market place', identical to its Surrey twin). Identical to Riverhead is **Rotherhithe** on the Surrey Thames. These places lie at either end of the long cattle-drove up from the Weald.

I must be reigned in, as I need to talk about town names. I said in Chapter 5 that the most obvious, staring regularity in Surrey town names is the linguistic element *ingas* : Godalming, Dorking, Woking. And so it is.

The celebrated case of *ingas*

Ingas, 'people', is a *cause célèbre* of English place-names. Thought once to indicate 'tribes' of early Anglo-Saxon colonists, it was realized subsequently not to correlate at all well with the locations of the earliest Anglo-Saxon cemeteries. Hmm, awkward. Surrey is a case in point; its aforesaid cemeteries are clustered in the north-east of the county, while *ingas* is almost exclusively a feature of west and central Surrey, especially the far south-west. Difficult.

Rather deflatingly, *ingas* was re-interpreted as a 'second phase' of Anglo-Saxon colonization, and unceremoniously dumped. Yet this particular element has popped up several times already in my narrative, *viz* : Getinges (**Eaton** in Cobham), Bintungom (**Binton** in **Seale**), **Dorking**, **Godalming**, **Woking**, **Eashing** and **Tooting**. Beyond Surrey too: at Barlings, Basing, Cooling, Eling, Epping, Exning, Goring,

Harting, Peppering and Poling. So what does *ingas* mean? The contexts have been variously Romano-British, pagan, Christian. Could this *ingas*, this 'people', hold the key to the shifting realities of the era? Certainly scholars have long thought so, and more recently there has been a reversion to the old 'tribal' model.

Luckily, I think I can claim to have solved the mystery. It is indeed to do with semantics. And date. And, yes, location.

Ingas and the Surrey hundreds

First, location. I have said *ingas* occurs in central and west Surrey. But also, it emerges, at *one per hundred,* as Figure 2 shows. **Godalming** and **Woking** name hundreds. **Dorking** is the economic focus of Wotton Hundred. When in the 680's Caedwalla founded Farnham minster, the latter was given Farnham Hundred as its territory, with its main estate named as Bintungom (ie. **Seale**). Similarly, in its nearly contemporary charter Chertsey Abbey was given Getinges (ie. **Cobham**) in Elmbridge Hundred. Of the only three other known *ingas* names in the county (though see Chapter 11 for an extra possibility), **Tyting** stands in for Blackheath Hundred. All these six hundreds abut each other; they fill up the whole of the south-western half of the county.

Eashing is unique in falling within another *ingas* hundred, Godalming, and indeed is only a mile from Godalming. **Tooting** in north-east Surrey is the other odd one out. We'll come back on these two later.

Who or what were the 'people'?

Fine, *ingas* occurs at one per hundred – one (with qualifications) per *every* hundred in the south-western half of the county. But not only that. These places were royal.

Godalming, Dorking and **Woking** all were royal estates, though at what date they were acquired is not known. **Eashing** clearly was a royal fortress. Bintungom was very likely royal given the name of its parish, **Seale**, which probably is *sele*, 'hall', rather than *sealh*, 'sallow-bush' (and anyway has a place called **Kingston** in it). This is a strong pattern. So let's assume for the moment that **Tyting**, Getinges and **Tooting** once also were royal, and see where that takes us.

Hundred centres, royal... The obvious assumption must be that these places were the political heart of each hundred, and that royalty acquired them because royalty wanted to control each and every district. Control the hundreds, and you control Surrey. But *who* were 'royalty'?

Next, date. The Chertsey and Farnham charters were written in the 670s and 680s respectively. So *ingas* is as old as that, but not necessarily much older; after all *ingas* does not appear any earlier in the *Anglo-Saxon Chronicle*. In the middle part of the seventh century, the royals running south-west Surrey were the royal families of Wessex. Surrey's *ingas* places could be the product – a rather formalized and regular product – of the kings of Wessex.

Now the final piece of the puzzle: semantics. What were the 'people' of, say, Godhelm up to in Godalming? Was Godhelm a local representative of Wessex royalty? The Venerable Bede is useful here, as ever. He may have lived a long way away and be a Northumbrian, but he's good on *ingas*. He deploys the term in several different ways. Writing in the 730s, he uses the rather archaic title 'Oiscingas' for the kings of Kent (Oisc being claimed as an early member), and 'Wuffingas' (*viz.* a supposed king Wuffa) for their East Anglian counterparts. I say 'archaic' because Bede is using *ingas* here in a way similar to that found in *Beowulf* – the first known epic poem in English, thought to be associated with the court of the part-pagan King Raedwald of East Anglia, *circa* 620. *Beowulf* describes Scandinavian tribes or warrior groups including the 'Scyldings', 'people of the shield', and the term 'Viking' is of this ilk. But these are not place-names, and Bede's usage elsewhere is different. In-Fippingum he refers to as the 'district' in which Bishop Diuma of Mercia died. But his In-Getlingum and his Barking specifically are monasteries.

Let's cut to the chase. *Ingas* is a pagan Scandinavian tribal and militaristic term, fashionable in East Anglia and Northumbria as a result of a renewed influx of Scandinavian colonists to at least East Anglia around 600 (the time of *Beowulf* and of Raedwald, who emerged briefly as East Anglia's only ever claim to over-kingship of Britain). The Northumbrian's picked up the habit because their future king, Edwin, spent time in his youth under Raedwald's protection (I'm getting most of this from Bede). Edwin then goes back up north and gets converted to Christianity by Paulinus, a companion of Augustine. But the Northumbrian Church evolves as a mixture of this papal Christianity plus Irish monasticism, because Paulinus having escaped south during a testing era, Edwin's successor Oswald invites Aidan abbot of the Irish monastery of Whithorn in Scotland to help out. Aidan becomes influential, as abbot of a new monastery set up at Lindisfarne on a typically remote 'Irish' site. And as Edwin was over-king, so too Oswald and his successor Oswy. Together, with set-backs, they bash up every heathen in sight and claim token control over most of Britain. Under them are sponsored the first bishops in most of the Anglo-Saxon kingdoms.

Across all this swathe of England under the control of Northumbria now spring up *local royal households in the guise of monasteries*, a hybrid of Irish monasticism and Anglo-Saxon militarism. My hypothesis is that many of these institutions are named in the Scandinavian formula *ingas*, in effect '(royal) household'. East Anglia in particular has a set of such names and places, including for example King Anna's estate at Exning and his monastery at Blythburgh in a hundred called Blything. Another probable monastery is Happisburgh, the focus of Happing Hundred. Not far to the west we find Barlings Abbey in Lincolnshire, and an important Romano-British religious centre focus in Hertfordshire renamed Braughing. Further, according to Bede, the mid seventh century was a period in which it becomes fashionable for Anglo-Saxon aristocrats to become monks, normally abbots; Bede says young nobs and old kings make it their business to go to Ireland for religious instruction, or else to abdicate and retire into a monastery.

All this might seem a trifle elaborate as an explanation. But if you think you are going to understand *ingas* without a passing knowledge of seventh-century political history, forget it. I'll press on.

Wessex and Birinus

Surrey at this time was much affected by Wessex. Wessex in 635 had received a fresh papal emissary, Birinus, made first bishop at Dorchester on Thames under the joint protection of Kings Cynegils of Wessex and Oswald of Northumbria. The Wessex of this era is spread with *ingas* places. They include the surviving early minster at **Wing** in Buckinghamshire, the monasteries of Sonning and Reading, the royal Hampshire estates Basing and Eling. And by tradition Birinus, or perhaps his successors at Dorchester, convert, or rather re-convert, Surrey.

I submit therefore that Surrey's *ingas* places are royal Wessex-sponsored monasteries, closely associated with the strategic royal holdings controlling each hundred. And that the period of their coining is between 635 and the 670s (for this latter date, see below). Which is nothing like either the traditional or the 'modern' explanation of *ingas*.

Dorking High Street. The town's name may contain a Celtic district name 'Dorce', perhaps referring to the vale of the Pipp Brook. Since Roman times a settlement here has been the economic focus of Wotton Hundred. The '-ing' part is *ingas*, 'people', revealing the parish church to be a mid-seventh-century minster. Thus do archaeology and place-names offer distinct but overlapping evidence.

Of course, all the above is speculation on my part. It well be wrong in its particulars, though I think the gist of it is right. Nor am I the first to unlock *ingas*, though the others didn't know they had. Ekwall says Berclingas (an early form for Berkeley in Gloucestershire) means 'the monks of Berkeley'. McNeil Dodgson thought a reference to 'Guthlacingas' to relate to the followers of Saint Guthlac, founder of Crowland Abbey in Lincolnshire *circa* 700. Both were spot on, I'd say.

But can the Surrey *ingas* places of Figure 2 be shown to be monastic? This is difficult, because John Blair claims the earliest Surrey church as Chertsey Abbey, founded in the 660s under Kent. I would challenge John. For a start, **Chertsey Abbey** probably is older (see below). But look to those *ingas* sites, they are very churchy. **Godalming** and **Woking** are known early minsters, and Blair says **Dorking** was likely a sub-minster. **Eashing**, perhaps 'people of the sacred ash-tree', is only a mile from **Peper Harow**, postulated as a regionally important pagan temple. **Tyting** likewise is sitting below **St Martha's Hill** with its chapel – a classic hill-top pagan site if ever there was one. Bintungom is perhaps similarly related to **Crooksbury Hill** (see Chapter 8). Which only leaves Getinges (**Cobham**) and **Tooting**. These I interpret as lost hundred focal monasteries thinned-out, like Tyting and Bintungom, in the minster reforms of the 670s (more on this below); both Getinges and Tooting were given to Chertsey Abbey in its charter of that age. So, potentially churches, or rather monasteries, all.

At a later date the remoter ex-pagan *ingas* sites, often on uncomfortable hill-tops, were dispensed with in favour of choicer marketable riverside sites. Sites like the new minster at **Farnham** to which Bintungom was referred, and **Godalming** ('Godhelm's *ingas*', a youngish-feeling name for an *ingas*) which takes over from nearby Eashing. This culling of pagan left-overs, occurring after the synods at Hertford and Hatfield (see below), could neatly unravel the puzzle of how *ingas* came to name on the one hand several towns, and on the other, remote farms like **Binton** in Seale, **Eaton** in Cobham, and **Tyting** in St Martha's. As the Church gives, so doth it take away. What it gives away as fast as it can in the late seventh century are any embarrassing hints of residual paganism. **Eashing/Peper Harow** had to go, and Bintungom/**Crooksbury** too. So too perhaps **Tooting**, which I have already suspected might refer to a sacred tumulus now lost, except Tooting's decline doubtless is due more to the rise of political power at Kingston upon Thames. **St Martha's** somehow survived, in spite of being as remote and pagan-looking as you could wish.

England's peripatetic early saints

Note that a majority of Surrey *ingas* place-names seem prefixed by a personal-name, a 'head of household'. Godhelm, Binta, Tyta, Wocc, Geat; rather like the Guthlac of Guthlacingas, or the Berica at Eorcenwold's sister's monastery of Barking. Were these fellows ecclesiastics, like Saint Guthlac? Probably so. As normal for the age, the majority of these ecclesiastics would have arisen from the aristocratic classes.

To my mind these named persons are late representatives of a system of local kingship in Britain dating from deep in prehistory, revived after the interlude of the Roman era, but about to be overtaken again by forces more powerful than itself. Caedwalla in 680s Wessex ended an era of 'sub-kings'. While it lasted this native British system, in some areas co-opted by local Germanic war-lords, perhaps earned the Germanic term *waru* ('people') – a term essential similar to *ingas* – either for the religious communities these individuals inspired, or for minor royalty's dependent subjects. This anyway is a possible interpretation of two contemporary references in ecclesiastical Latin: Bede's 'Meanuarum provincia' for the people of the valley of the river Meon (a Celtic name) not far away in Hampshire, and Symeon of Durham's 'Hestingorum gens' for the Hastings area in Sussex. Here perhaps are hundred-level political units, about to be lost to history. Other examples of *waru* seemingly referring to a political hundred or its central, now monastic community are the hill-top 'Clifwara' at Clewer by Windsor, and 'Clifwara' at Cliffe by Halstow; whereas in 'Cantwara' we are dealing with a political community of city-state dimensions at Canterbury. No name of leader, whether kinglet or abbot (except in the case of Kent and Canterbury) has come down to us; their place was to slide from history, until revived by the Norman baronetcy (though some major Anglo-Saxon thanes may locally have filled the political vacuum).

Godhelm of Godalming has disappeared into the mists of time, no less than the presumed pagan priest Cusa of *Cusan weoh*, perhaps a near neighbour. Some had more staying-power. Binta reappears fourteen miles from Bintungom, at Bentworth over the Hampshire border. Wocc similarly appears sixteen and again twenty-four miles from Woking, at Wokingham and Wokefield in Berkshire. Might this indicate that the spheres of influence of Bintungom's and Woking's centres once were double or more in size? Did relatively peaceful times from the late seventh century allow population growth and the budding-off of daughter institutions? Perhaps.

A variant explanation is suggested by Sunna of Sonning near Reading. He seems to pop up again at both Sunbury in Middlesex and Sunningwell below Boar's Hill by Abingdon. If this really is the same person, these latter place-names tend to confirm the notion that he was a peripatetic priest: an English equivalent of Bishop Teilo of South Wales with his various Llandeilo and Llantilio. Sunningwell probably was a monastic community at a holy well; Sunbury (as we shall see) may contain *burh* in the sense 'monastery'. Later I shall postulate one Tilla at **Shere**. If he existed did he embrace also Tilbury ('Tilla's *burh* ') in Essex, a monastery cited by Bede, and **Tillingdown** (now naming a farm in Tandridge Hundred in east Surrey but assessed by John Blair to be originally the name of the hill-top church of **Tandridge** itself, a difficult name containing 'ridge')? Or was there more than one Tilla?

Maybe Godhelm was local equivalent of the three persons – indubitably priests – into whose care Farnham minster was assigned in its charter of *circa* 685: Cedde, Cisi and Criswa. To *Place-Names* these individuals are 'otherwise unknown'. My guess is Cisi names also the cathedral site Chichester. Ekwall notes that a Cissa was son to fifth-century over-king Aelle of Sussex; perhaps this simply confirms (as indeed the king-lists show) that royals liked to keep certain names in the family. The same aristocratic, peripatetic ecclesiastic may have owned a stopping-off pad on the Chichester-to-London road at Cisendune (**Chessington**) on a stretch diverted from its original Roman alignment by the emerging attractions of Kingston upon Thames.

Yet far and away the most exciting manhunt concerns Basa or Bass. He of Basing by Basingstoke, not a million miles from Surrey. Could this be the 'thane Bassus' whom Bede records as fleeing from Yorkshire to Rochester with Bishop Paulinus in 633? Or the 'mass-priest Bass' the *Anglo-Saxon Chronicle* says was given Reculver for a monastery by King Egbert of Kent in 669? This late minutiae from Kent, unusual for the *Chronicle*, strongly suggests Bass cut ice in Wessex. My guess is yes, they all are one and the same person. Furthermore, Besingahearh, royal signing-place of the Farnham minster charter, might well be Basing, *hearg* here in a sunset semantic as '(Christian) temple'.

Tooting in north-east Surrey on the other hand may be part of a scattered group of *ingas* places in the London area, with Barking, Yeading, Ealing. Conceivably these were communities established by

Bishop Wini, kicked out of Wessex after a row with his king but 'buying' (as Bede says) the bishopric of London from the Mercians. Or is their date earlier, forming part of an East Saxon set including Epping, Ingatestone, Nazeing, Barling, Wakering? These possibly date from the time of Cedd, first bishop at Bradwall on Sea in the 650s, whose influence may have reached the London area.

Each set of *ingas* names has its own history, essentially to do with the *diocese* in which they arise. Had I more time I would investigate the *ingas* swarm in Sussex, and its likely connection with the Northumbrian Wilfrid and his late conversion of the South Saxons in the 680s; or *ingas* on the Medway, and its connection with the destruction of the cathedral and churches of the Rochester diocese during a messy invasion by Mercians described by Bede for 676, and their likely subsequent resuscitation and renaming by Caedwalla and his now mentor the same Wilfrid after the latter's invasion of Kent a decade later (Caedwalla's pilgrimage to Rome, followed).

But I should mention the Continental place-names that appear to be equivalents of *ingas* (Ekwall cites from Germany Sigmaringen, 'Sigimar's people', and perhaps could have cited Bingen or Singen). There is no necessary reason for their semantics to be the same as England's; they might retain the original 'tribal' semantic. Or indeed they might be exports from England, taken with the English missionaries of the seventh century, including Wilfrid, whom Bede records as braving the pagans of Frisia and Saxony.

-inga- names

A last point. Any theory of *ingas* has to cope with place-names the like of Besingaheah containing *-inga-*, the genitive form of *ingas*. Abingdon, **Artington** (Hertindon), **Tillingdown** and **Chessington** (Cisendune) we have come across, all paired with *dun*, 'hill', and Sunningwell (and we shall check out **Tillingbourne**) paired with *wielle* (or *burna*), 'spring'. The *hearg* of Besingaheah indubitably is religious; it is found not only at **Peper Harow** but at Harrow on the Hill in Middlesex, the blatantly pagan-originating hill-top church site known formerly as *Gumeninga herg,* suggested by Coates to be 'the peoples' temple' (though 'the Lord's temple' is an option). *Dun* in the case of Abingdon (a name relating to Boar's Hill, where the abbey is said first to have been located), Hertindon (**St Catherine's Hill**), and Tillingdown (if **Tandridge**) may allow *–ingadun* a sense '(religious) community on the (sacred) hill'. Do not such names mark the Christian take-over of sacred pagan hill-tops? Certainly the *Life* of Saint Cuthbert mentions an 'oratory', perhaps hilltop chapel, of the Abbess of Whitby at a place called Osingadun.

Sunningwell could be at a sacred spring on the slopes of Boar's Hill; Tillingbourne I shall posit as linking the Silent Pool to a lost 'Tilling'. My point is that several types of *-inga-* name perhaps fit easily into an ecclesiastical model of *ingas*. And then there is Ivinghoe Beacon on the scarp of the Chilterns, an *-ingahoh* name that might neatly introduce Chapter 12.

And I ought to mention the distinctive set of large Surrey Wealden parishes with *-inga-* names: **Blechingley**, **Lingfield** (not definitely an *-inga-* name), **Abinger** and **Chiddingfold**. There, *-inga-* status conceivably relates directly to early status as embryonic parish, as might be suggested also for a Wilfridian wash of late *ingas* estate names in Sussex. Similar might be said of certain north Surrey *ham* names with *-inga-* which invariably become parishes: **Effingham**, **Warlingham**, **Woldingham**, a lost Washingham (an old name for either Clapham or Wandsworth) and perhaps a lost Tillingaham (see Chapter 12). So again, *ingas* and *-inga-* may well refer to 'people' specifically in their *religious* aspect.

12. Chertsey and the minster reforms

Wind forward in time to the last days of *ingas*. The termination of *ingas* occurred, I suspect, when this odd English hybridization of the Irish monastic movement and the Germanic aristocratic household was routed by the young Wilfrid's Romanist arguments at the synod of Whitby in 664, and by the Roman reforms consolidated by Archbishop Theodore at the synods of Hertford and Hatfield in 673 and 680. Consequent upon these events, the Irish monks took their ball home and left England to the papists. *Ingas*-naming died with them.

Irish-style foundations are conveniently to be dubbed *monasteries* rather than minsters; they had a less formal role in local administration. The Irish style of organization was looser, and quite probably had roots in the pagan Druidic colleges associated with Celtic aristocracies. By contrast the Roman-style *minster* (as I shall call it – the scribes of the various versions of the *Chronicle* are less consistent in their definitions) was styled upon the late Roman Empire, and administered along strict hierarchical and territorial lines. The story of the seventh century Church in England is that of the rivalry between these two traditions. As usual, the Romans won. By the end of the century Roman-style minsters were established throughout under a new Mercian *bretwalda*; and the thumb-print of the Church got all over the lists of English place-names. Surrey is no exception. The most famous of its names is Chertsey. But the roots went deeper.

'Cerot's island'

Chertsey Abbey was Surrey's most important early church. None other than the Venerable Bede himself explains the meaning of its name, but his explanation is enigmatic. He goes out of his way to explain that Cerotaesei is 'Cerot's island'. He does not explain Cerot, a Celtic personal-name. He does not explain 'island'.

If his readers were familiar with that second-element (normally given as *eg)*, why bother to explain it? Almost no other place-name does he explain – but there are exceptions. Adbaruae, In-Derawuda, Maildufi urbs, Tunnacaestir. William of Malmesbury explains Maildulf (Irish Maelduib) as a Scot – i.e. Irishman – who founded Malmesbury Abbey.

In the case of Tunnacaestir, Bede says specifically it is a monastery founded by abbot Tunna. This last must be at a Roman site, a Roman *castra*, as was Andredescester (another name for Pevensey). Yes, *urbs* is Latin for 'town', and *ceaster* from Latin *castra* a defended site (our 'castle'); but in all instances Bede is explaining the name of a *monastery*. The point is that, like *urbs* and *ceaster*, *eg* had evolved into a term specifically for a monastery: *eg* might be literally 'island', but is euphemistically an 'isolated retreat'. We use 'island' in this sense today. This is I think how his contemporary ecclesiastical readers would have read him, and what he intended.

There is a case to answer that *eg* means monastery because so many monasteries were called it. Romsey, Ramsey, Muchelney, Athelney (King Alfred's hiding-place), Bardney, Partney, Selsey (Wilfrid's cathedral), and more. Thorney Abbey is in Cambridgeshire, but the name recurs at Westminster and also formerly in Suffolk at Stou (*stow*, 'sacred meeting-place', now Stowmarket). *Eg* is assumed by Gelling and Cole in topographic mode to be 'dry ground in a marsh'. Islands that may have monasteries on them (Sheppey, Lundy, Bardsey, Anglesea, Jersey) are dismissed as mere islands. But is there more to it? Barrie Cox in his study of the earliest place-names, clearly observes that *eg* names 'large estates' up to the eighth century but not thereafter. Curious. Curiouser, as Alice might have said, *eg* is appended to the names of major monasteries in the seventh century but later dropped. This occurred at Glastonbury (Glastingaea/Glastingei in 704 and 744), Hartlepool (Bede's Heruteu/Herutei/Heruteig), Hexham (Hagustaldes ea in 681), Lastingham (Bede's Laestingaeu) and the British minster of St Nectan's at Hartland in Devon (Heortigtun, *circa* 880). Curiouser still, *eg/eu/ei/eig/ea* has for Bede no agreed spelling, and by implication no agreed pronunciation.

That *eg* might actually be *Irish*, adapted via Irish-Northumbrian monasticism in the English Age of Saints as 'monastic retreat', is suggested to me by a name for Iona, '*I Columb-kill*, i.e. 'the island of (Saint) Columb's cell'. But whatever its origin, it is clear to me at least that *eg* is a word used in the early period – and *only* in this period – for 'monastery'. Later, the word (or a similar Germanic or Celtic one) reverts simply to 'island', as in the dialect eyot/ait for small islands in the Surrey Thames. If so, the usage of *eg* parallels that of Welsh *llan* in the Age of Saints as '(monastic) enclosure', with its subsequent reversion to its prior meaning 'enclosure'. Similarly again, Scandinavian *holms* ('small island') appears in the name of monastic sites in northern and eastern England, as at Hulme St Benet in Norfolk, Holme Cuttram in Cumbria, and at Durham Cathedral which is *dun holms* ('hill island', and well inland).

Exactly when British or Irish clerics were present at any particular English monastery is difficult to know. Bede cites a small Irish monastery at Bosham in Sussex *circa* 680. John Morris cites an Irish tradition of Aben founding Abingdon Abbey in the late sixth century. Abingdon, its name and monastery subsequently relocated off Boar's Hill, illustrates perhaps archetypally the genesis of an *-ingadun* place-name: 'the (sacred) hill of Aben's (monastic) community'. I suspect Cerot, like Aben, may have been Irish.

Battersea, Molesey, Titsey

If one suspects *eg* names hide early churches of significance, then think Eye, Rye, Eyam, Olney. But Surrey too is a good place for *eg* hunting. **Chertsey Abbey** we know, and Chertsey is only the most prestigious of a string of *eg* estates along the Surrey Thames.

Bermondsey is a known monastery from the early eighth century. **Battersea** was a large estate, in 693 a possession of Bishop Eorcenwold, and had in its Celtic-named estate **Penge** (that is *pen coed*, either 'end of wood' or 'chief wood') a holding just over the Kent border: aspects that might imply a late-seventh century status as minster, or ex-minster, in this case of Brixton Hundred. (On the transient or potential minsters of this lamentable hundred, too close to London for its own good, see my comments elsewhere on Southwark, Tooting, Wimbledon and Merton.)

Molesey is interesting in that while Chertsey has its Cerot and Bermondsey its Beornmund (both I suspect early abbots), Molesey has Mul. Mul ('mule', that is 'half-breed', perhaps 'half Welsh') by coincidence or otherwise was the name of King Caedwalla's brother, with whom he went raiding into Kent and the Isle of Wight in 686, as the *Chronicle* proudly reports. When in the next year Mul was burned alive by naughty Kentishmen, Caedwalla went on the rampage again. Had Mul in the meantime done a typical aristocratic about-turn, and become abbot at Molesey? Such things did happen in the seventh century.

Well away from the Thames, away indeed from any islands or any marshes, is **Titsey** by Limpsfield. Tita's *eg.* Titsey is excellent evidence that *eg* does not mean 'dry land in a marsh'. As yet there is no evidence that there was an early monastery here either, but it may be discovered one day, probably not far from the Romano-British temple at the source of the Eden. At least, that's my bet.

Burh as monastery

The term for 'monastery' used colloquially among later seventh-century and eighth-century monkish communities was neither *ingas* nor *eg*, but *burh*. Or *ceaster*. Or (in ecclesiastical Latin) *urbs*. Thus Bede's 'Maildulfi urbs' for Malmesbury Abbey, his explanation of the name Tunnacaestir, and his statement concerning the great Welsh monastery of Bangor-is-y-Coed 'which the English call Bancornaburg'.

Burh is a direct parallel to Welsh *llan*, since it originally meant something like 'defensible enclosure'. Much the same meaning in fact as *ceaster*. All were used in the seventh century, I suggest, for monastic enclosures. Pretty much equivalent is our term cathedral 'close', but relevant also is the embankment Bede (book 4, ch. 28) describes Saint Cuthbert erecting around his tiny solitary hermitage on Farne Island, an embankment 'so high that he could see nothing but the heavens for which he longed so ardently'.

This interpretation is not wildly counter-intuitive for *burh*, since *burh* occurs in English monastic names even more often than *eg*, sometimes in places where no alternative explanation as 'fort' or 'town' is tenable. (John Blair agrees – personal communication; as does Michael Swanton in his introduction to the Phoenix edition of the *Anglo-Saxon Chronicle*). Likely suspects include Malmesbury, Glastonbury (Glestingabyrig, 732–55), plus East Anglian names often in -burgh (Tasburgh, Mickleburgh, Dickleburgh, Attleborough, Aldeburgh, Sudbury, etc.) and a rash of Wessex names in -bury (Westbury, Henbury, Banbury, Shaftesbury, Ramsbury, Charlbury, Bibury, Tetbury, etc.). Blatant are Bury St Edmunds, Peterborough ('St Peter's'), and 'Paulus byrig aet Lundaenae' for St Paul's. Elsewhere in this book we find Happisburgh, Blythburgh, Sunbury, Tilbury. And for good measure I'll chuck in Canterbury (perhaps '[main] minster' rather than 'fort' of Kent) and Salisbury. The latter was called Searobyrg by the *Chronicle* referring to the year 552 when Old Sarum was a vast hill fort not yet adapted to minster town, but the record dates from the ninth century, but which time it was.

Perhaps the best evidence that a particular *burh* name refers to a monastery rather than a 'fort' or 'manor' is when it has a personal-name qualifier. I have revealed my preference for seeing Cerot as abbot. Maelduib certainly was. Similar applies to Dicul at Dickleburgh, whom Tom Williamson probably correctly identifies with the Irishman Dicul a companion of the missionary Fursey in the 630s. Tette, sister of King Ine (reigned 688–726), was Abbess of Wimbourne, and likely also of Tetbury. Bede reckons Bamburgh Castle was named from Bebbe, Queen of King Aethelfrith (reigned 593–616). Bibury was given, doubtless as a monastery, to earl Leppa's daughter Beage, sometime between 721 and 743. It's good to see the women getting a look in.

The 'old *burh*' phenomenon

There seem no potential examples of monastic *burh* in Surrey, other than **Burstow** already mentioned. Normally *burh* in Surrey means 'hill-fort', as at **Anstiebury** ('fort by the single-track') or **Holmbury** (perhaps 'the fort in the Holmwood') or the no longer interpretable names associated with 'Caesar's' two Camps by Wimbledon ('Bensbury' in the sixteenth century) and Farnham (on **Bricksbury Hill**), or is 'manor' as in **Norbury** ('north estate'). But what of the parish name **Albury**, 'old *burh*', whose land encompasses the Sherbourne spring?

Albury is, I suggest, one of a group of names to set alongside the more prestigious Aldeburgh in Suffolk. Normally, equivalent names in Surrey are assumed to refer to left-over Iron Age hill forts, and in some cases this may be correct. But not always. This is clear from the records of the gaunt ruins of Newark Priory on the River Wey, founded *circa* 1190, and described in 1210 as *novo locus de Andebir*, 'the new site of the old monastery'. Blair, probably correctly, thinks the old monastery in question was the former minster of Woking.

At Albury, was the pagan magic of the Silent Pool sufficient to attract a Christian monastery, one forgotten but hinted at by the parish name? Indeed its site may have been where now stands the half-ruined Saxon parish church. This site must have become 'old' when superseded by the sub-minster at Shere.

Which leads me to yet another candidate. St Ann's Hill formerly was known as 'Eldebury'. Eldebury *might* mean the hill-fort here, but could just as easily refer the site of the chapel of St Ann's within it. I muse that if this chapel, a hill-top oratory, marks the original site of Chertsey Abbey, then could 'Chertsey' have ended up as 'Chertingdon'? Cisi after all may have generated both a 'Chichester' and a 'Cissingadun'. Had we been in Wales, 'Chertsey' might instead be 'Llangerot'.

The earliest churches of England

To recap. I propose **Chertsey** started life as a Celtic-style monastery. This is the logical explanation for its Celtic-named Cerot, who would have been an early abbot. The abbey by the end of the seventh century doubled as a Roman-style minster, but its history would seem to be shared with the Celtic abbeys of Glastonbury, Abingdon, Malmesbury and Shaftsbury. Each originally occupied a spectacular pagan hill top site: Glastonbury Tor, Boar's Hill, the high river-cliffs of Malmesbury and Shaftsbury, plus **St Ann's Hill**. In several cases the memory of an Irish 'founder' (in reality, re-founder) is preserved.

These monasteries survived one way or another the pagan revivals of the early seventh century. As we know from Ely, not all had it easy. But pagan-*cum*-Christian sites seem to have had tenacious hold on local communities and frequently were revived. The tendency of churches to be re-founded on former religious sites has indeed been elevated into a model by G.Rosser (in J.Blair and C.Pyrah, *Church Archaeology*, 1996). Some early monasteries, like Chertsey, were re-founded as the new minsters in Theodore's centralising reforms; many got weeded out. Celtic-style oratories became *outré*, though not quite totally. Glastonbury Tor retained its chapel; so too St Ann's Hill, where remained a healing well and a mythical stone. And come to that, **St Catherine's Chapel** on 'dragon's hill', once Hertindon. Later on, the minsters themselves slipped from centre stage as the bishops strengthened their hold, feudal lords favoured new-fangled Norman-French monastic orders and ostentatious estate churches, and guilds did the same in the burgeoning medieval cities and wool towns.

Sir Frank Stenton has suggested that many humble parish churches may hide former monasteries. We can now see that for many of these, their names give them away. Olney, Rye, Reading, Goring, Blythburgh, Bibury. **Chertsey**, **Dorking**, **Albury**, **Shere**. The lost monastic and minster names of England, no less than our pagan names, are overdue for rehabilitation.

12. Shapeshifting: the several names of Kingston-upon-Thames

A curious fact has arisen more than once in this book: that **Kingston-upon-Thames** seems to have had several previous names. In sum, they are Freoricburna, Moreford and Waleport. Waleport we have met; it seems to be a memory of a Romano-British urban settlement. Moreford too; this is the name said in Tudor times to have been the town's former name. It sounds like a standard-issue London Basin central-place name reflecting Kingston's location and importance as river-crossing (either of the Thames, or the lost Winchester Road's crossing of the river Hogs Mill). Freoricburna is courtesy of John Blair; this is a royal signing place appearing on Mercian charters that disappears when'Kingston' starts to be mentioned, so Blair suggests it *is* Kingston. It has the ring of a monastic name, '(At) the priest Freoric's sacred spring'; quite likely there was a royal monastery at Kingston's now demolished Anglo-Saxon coronation chapel of St Mary. Thus do Kingston's past names record the shifting cultural shapes of what essentially has been a single central place throughout history.

Relict place-name clusters

Yet it turns out that Kingston Hundred and its focus is not at all unusual in this regard. Most Surrey hundreds show a similar *cluster of relict place-names* associated with the past locations and functions of their central place. One rich source of multiple names is the dichotomy of secular and religious centre in earlier times; another is the shift from remote pagan sites to more marketable Christian ones.

Had I the space I would treat you to a comprehensive listing of Surrey's hundredal place-name clusters as I see them. As it is, you will have to do that work yourself. I will merely give you a few clues.

Start with all the *ingas* names, and all occurrences of pre-Germanic elements (though leave out the widespread *patois* of *ford, dun, cumb* and *stret,* and the possibly antique *ora*). I have given you a kick start with Figure 2 which offers a base map for this purpose. Include also all *hoh* names. Personally I suspect *hoh* may relate not (as Gelling and

Cole suggest) simply to 'heel-shaped (hills)', but perhaps to the lop-sided profile of the typical ancestral long barrow (though few survive in Surrey), or to a ramped moot mound (one possible candidate being 'The Mount' at **Barrow Green** in Tandridge Hundred). My reason? The stand-alone name **Hoe** (*hoh*) occurs in Surrey only in the *ingas* parishes of Godalming (where there is also a **Munstead**, which could be a related name 'mount place'), Woking and Dorking and near Gomshall (for all of which see below) but elsewhere at Hoo in Kent as Halstow ('holy place') and more famously at the Germanic burial site of Sutton Hoo in Raedwald territory. Was *hoh*, with *ingas*, the first Germanic term applied to hundred foci in west Surrey? The secular core, paralleling the religious?

Try also 'shambles' names (*sceamol*, ostensibly 'shelf, bench'), as these might relate to temporary features erected at hundred moots or courts, or indeed to permanent mounds there; there is a Shamel Hundred in Kent. In Surrey Motshambles, 'the moot benches', at a junction of several lanes, was a meeting-place of Copthorne Hundred. Dorking has two separate *sceamol* farm names, while **Shamley Green** lies close to Blackheath; both localities were hundred foci. Add 'staple' names if you like; *stapol* likely meant 'pillar' and names several hundreds elsewhere. Recorded are 'La Stapele in Shyre' (Shere; now **Stapleland Copse**) and a 'Simon ate Stapele' in Horley (in Crutchfield territory; recalled in **Staplehurst Farm**).

Some hundredal clusters have already been touched upon in Farnham Hundred (**Crooksbury/Seale/Binton/Kingston**) and Reigate Hundred (**Crutchfield/Thunderfield/Lowfield/Burstow/Horleyland**). Over in Kent we saw Hoo/Cooling/Halstow. Clusters offer a way of identifying the one-time central places of lost hundreds, too – as at **Titsey/Limpsfield**.

Ingas is particularly fruitful in all this. If *ingas* initially named a royal household rather than a site *per se*, an earlier site name reasonably might survive in tandem with an *ingas* name; thus **Crooksbury**, **Peper Harow** and **St Martha's** each may be the earlier name of the sacred place (in Farnham and Godalming Hundreds and the Guildford area). In a way, the most remarkable thing about those transient pieces of social history the *ingas* names, is that they survived at all. Maybe they survived, together with some old pagan names, because of the political economic astuteness of royal families who muscled in on hundred centres but then moved said centres to new riverside, future urban sites (a fair proportion of them doubtless close to former Roman minor central places) leaving the post-Roman cult sites to moulder half forgotten, except as place-names.

I may actually have spotted a lost *ingas* name. *Place-Names* cites a 'Tyllingeham' in the Assize Roll for **Shere** manor; clearly associated is the name of the river **Tillingbourne**, but also that of **Tenningshook Wood** ('Tilling's *hoc*') in Shere parish, and perhaps also the local surname Tilling. Was 'Tilling' an interim seventh-century royal monastic name at **Albury** (rather as Getinges was at **Cobham**), with Tillingaham its subsidiary farmstead or off-shoot (rather as Wokingham was subsidiary to **Woking**), sited at Shere to which the minster and its original 'nature name' re-located? If so, Tillingbourne is either 'the river at Tillingham', or else is yet another name for the **Silent Pool**, 'the spring of Tilla'. Perhaps the relocation to Tillingham/Shere relates to the adjacent royal estate of **Gomshall** – especially if the latter's name 'guma's *scelf* (a parallel to Gumeninga hearg at Harrow on the Hill) means the 'shelf' of the 'peoples'/lord's (mound)' at the hundred moot, marked perhaps also by **Hoe** nearby. Guesswork, only guesswork, though a jolly good potential cluster.

Gelling and Cole think *scelf* refers simply to 'level ground', and they might be right. It possibly reoccurs in the difficult name **Horsell** (unless here is the equally interesting *(ge)sele*, 'shelter'). Horsell lies close to **Hoe** in **Woking**, in Woking Hundred, and its church stands invitingly upon a hill. I am only half-convinced by my lines of reasoning here. *Place-Names* says Horsell means 'dirty shelf', which reminds me of my garden shed. But perhaps yet another cluster?

Opposite: The now disused parish church of **Albury**. Does the name mean 'old minster', and was the church founded as a monastery close to the once-sacred **Silent Pool**? The pool's earlier name is preserved in the adjacent **Sherbourne Farm** (*scir burna*, '?clear spring'), but was later transferred to Blackheath Hundred's new minster at **Shere** a mile away. This cluster of relict central-place names at the heart of a hundred may include also the river name **Tillingbourne**, the village name **Gomshall**, and another local place-name **Hoe**.

13. Send, a root name

Since we are English, we like to assume our place-names are in English. A lot of them are, but many others aren't. Some are *translations* into English. The rather obscure parish name **Send** can be used to exemplify what is going on. At the same time we can clear up a last group of English place-name suffixes: *dun, stede* and *tun*.

The place-names of the *Anglo-Saxon Chronicle*

I am not sure if anyone else has pointed out that the place-names of the first 200 years of the 'English' records of the *Anglo-Saxon Chronicle* (i.e. from Hengest's arrival in 449, up until the later seventh century) are significantly different from those that come after. A large proportion are *Romano-British*, in more or less garbled form. Bear in mind we are talking about 200 years, not some brief transient era. Two hundred years is *eight generations*. We know from our own times that speech can change quite a bit even in even one generation. So there was no rush into Anglo-Saxon 'English'. People were still using versions of Romano-British place-names for a long time, and only from the later seventh century do ecclesiastical land charters appear using 'standard' English place-name types.

The Celtic base-line

Some kind of Celtic base line is obvious from very existence of Cædwalla in the 680s, and a late Celtic place-name like Liss. There is also **Penge**, now officially in Kent but once an outlier of the Battersea estate. This again is pure, post-Roman *Welsh*, that is *pen cet*, 'chief (or, the end of the) wood', identical to Pencoyd in Herefordshire, Penketh in Lancashire, Pencoed in Glamorgan.

Other direct evidence is provided by the north Surrey set of *wealh* ('foreigner/Briton/slave', our 'Welsh') place-names. These I suggest refer to '*Welsh-speakers*'. Indeed Michael Wood thinks Celtic may have been spoken on the Hampshire Downs into medieval times. Kenneth Cameron thought *wealh* place-names showed that in north Surrey the Britons and Anglo-Saxons long lived in close proximity and he assumed, harmony. Interestingly enough, the settlements in question are cheek by jowl with (in fact sometimes *are*) the local central places: *viz.* **Walworth** (by Southwark), Waleport (at or by Kingston upon Thames), **Walton on Thames** (a sub-minster site in Elmbridge Hundred), **Wallington** (naming Croydon's hundred) and by Chertsey, Wealas huthe and Wealagate that appear in the abbey's land charters of the 670s. The *tun* (see below) in some of these names tends to confirm a late seventh-century date. Their location, hard up against the county's main central places, is reminiscent of the 'native quarters' of Indian cities familiar to historians of the British Raj. Did 'Welsh' people collect by these nascent towns because British-speakers were the original population anyway, or because they were the general populace attracted in from the surrounding countryside – or both?

Language change

Such observations offer the possibility that the changeover from Celtic to English in Surrey was a long-winded process. A corollary is that there may survive more Celtic place-names than we know. Richard Coates has re-assessed **Leatherhead**, **Merrow** and **Coulsdon** as Celtic. There are in addition a number of other place-names which *Place-Names* found difficult or on which Ekwall demurs. Names like **Merstham**, **Tandridge**, **Esher**, **Wimbledon**, **Sheen**, **Mortlake**, and maybe **Wanborough**, **Reigate** and **Lingfield**. Names with no very clear Germanic explanation (though sometimes I may have chanced my own explanations).

We know there was bilingualism, with Celtic and Anglo-Saxon spoken in parallel. I have alluded to Bede's reference in the 730s to the Welsh monastery of Bangor-is-Coed 'which the English call Bancornaburg'. An ecclesiastical Latin record of 682 states of Creechbarrow in Somerset: *collem qui dicitur britannica ligua Cructan apud nos Crycbeorh*, that is 'the mount called in British Cructan, but by us Creechbarrow'. The 'us' are English-speakers, but the ecclesiastical scribe writes in Latin and apparently has an acquaintance with Celtic. Creechbarrow is identical to the Surrey place-name **Crooksbury**. We must therefore assume bilingualism was present also in Surrey. In other words, *English was not the unchallenged national language*.

We know also that some Latin and Celtic terms were taken up into the English place-name canon. This we could assume reflects either imperial entities (such as *stret, port*) or traditional native entities (*cruc, funta, ford* and, for a brief while, *ora*) still functioning into Anglo-Saxon times, and perhaps other Celtic-derived terms could be interpreted in this light. More radically, let me suggest that these borrowed terms found in early English place-names are *patois*. That Surrey went through a period – say 400–600 – when some sort of *Celtic-Germanic patois* developed, probably in the north-east Surrey zone of cultural mixing, subsequently giving way to pure English, but preserved in place-names surviving from that era.

It's time to face up to England's linguistic history in an open and honest way. This chapter, from a place-names studies point of view – indeed, from a social history point of view – is, barring the *next* chapter, the core of this book.

Root names

Englishness cannot be taken for granted. *Linguistic layering*, if I can invent that term, can sometimes – in fact can often – be found within a single place-name. **Limpsfield** and **Crooksbury** are examples, part-Celtic, part-Germanic. Place-name studies have tended to focus on the typical suffixes that so many English place-names display – the '-ham','-stead ','-ing ','-ley' and so on – and paid less regard than they should to the first-elements of names. They have thereby missed the option of examining language layers. Furthermore, they seem not to have noticed that quite a high proportion of English place-names have a '*root-name*', as we might call it, quite independent of any suffix. One way into this issue is to look at a name without any suffix.

Look at Send and at Ash. These names are single-element. However, they are paralleled by others elsewhere in Surrey possessing a variety of endings. Thus for west Surrey's **Send** ('sandy place'), see east Surrey's **Sandown** (with suffix *dun*), **Sanderstead** (with *stede*, or possibly *hamstede*), and **Santon** in Reigate (with *tun*). For west Surrey's **Ash** ('ash-tree') and **Eashing** (*ingas*), see east Surrey's **Ashtead** (*stede*) and outside Surrey, Ashton (*tun*). The meanings of these two sets (with the partial exception of the *ingas* name) are much of muchness. In other words, the choice of suffix does not really affect the meaning. Sandown, Sanderstead and Santon each are upon hills; any one of them might have been called Sandown with *dun* for 'hill/hill settlement' (see below); any of them could have been called Sanderstead or Santon, both *stede* and *tun* meaning no more than 'estate', 'place', or at best 'settlement'. The reason, let me suggest, they got different endings is solely because they were named by *different agencies* – normally in different eras, often in different districts. Place-names like 'sandy-place', and perhaps 'place of the (sacred) ash-tree', work in this way because they are place-name roots likely to recur in Surrey. For another potential example see 'place of the oak-tree', as in **Ockford, Ockley, Oxted, Ockham, Oxshott, Oakwood** (though some of these place-names are said to contain the personal-names Occa or Ocga).

Dun and the *patois* era

Wimbledon, if Wibbandun, is the earliest recorded Surrey place-name. Excellent if you like tennis. There may be no coincidence Wibbandun is a *dun* name. *Dun*, I suggest, forms the earliest type of 'English' place-name, even though it is Celtic. Or more properly, *patois*.

Does *dun* occurs where it does because the earliest Anglo-Saxon speakers here lived as close neighbours to native British settlements? The Anglo-Saxons and Britons referred to settlements by the natives' words, in this case a version of Romano-British –*dunon* (as in Roman Camulodunon, Colchester) which in parallel became Welsh *dinas*, 'hill-fort'. Gelling has proposed, probably correctly, that although *dun* came in English to mean 'hill' (our 'downland'), its original meaning was 'British hill village'. In Surrey, as Figure 3a illustrates, *dun* place-names are markedly concentrated in a band across the north-east of the county close to the earliest Germanic cemeteries: **Wimbledon, Malden** (Meldon at Domesday), **Morden** (Mordone at Domesday), **Chessington** (Cisendune at Domesday), **Coulsdon,** and the non-parish names **Sandown, Selsdon, Waddon**. Most of them are on low hills, but not necessarily all.

They may be on hills for good reason. In the troubled times at the close of the Roman Empire in Britain, just before the era in which these *dun* names were perhaps coined, it was a good idea to live on a hill. Hills are easier to defend, whereas rivers and rich valley lands invite unwelcome guests. I have already suggested a parallel process, the blossoming importance of the Weald – a native retreat on a grander geographical scale.

Dun seems to me to track this two-fold phenomenon: a British retreat to local hill sites, and contact with neighbouring Anglo-Saxons. North-east Surrey was only one such theatre: others *dun* zones lay north of Birinus' cathedral at Dorchester on Thames, and in Northumbria near Bede's monastery at Jarrow on Tyneside. But this was not the case over the rest of Surrey, where *dun* (except in its later semantic as 'downland', as at **Highdown** and **Houndown**) scarcely occurs. Clearly the pattern bears no relation to Surrey's distribution of hills *per se*, or of villages on hills. Westerly or southerly exceptions are widely spaced, at **Worplesdon** ('hill with a trackway'), **Hambledon** ('broken hill'), **Clandon** ('clean down'), **Chaldon** ('calves' down'), and here *dun* seems to have a meaning intermediate between 'hill village' and simply 'hill' or 'downland'; the date may be seventh century, as the last two names appear in the Chertsey charter of the 670s.

Stede in east Surrey

East Surrey *stede* parish names like **Ashtead**, **Sanderstead** or **Oxted** are scarcely less interesting. *Stede* is pure Germanic: our word 'stead' (i.e. 'standing'), or 'steading' (a word for farmstead). It is related to the words '-stow' and '-stock', with little to distinguish their meanings.

The earliest record of '-stead' may be east Surrey's **Chipstead**, again from the Chertsey charter. Seemingly, *stede* is a parallel to that equally Germanic formula, north Surrey's *ham*, and could have been in fashion either before or after *ham*. But *stede* is distinct from *ham* in rarely having a personal-name first-element (though **Walkingstead**, the old name for Godstone, may be 'Wolcan's *stede*'). Sometimes a 'nature' or farming first-element reiterates those of single-element west Surrey names (such as Ash, Send, 'Oak-') that we shall shortly characterise as direct translations from Celtic. Could *stede* represent a first re-branding of east Surrey British estates into Germanic terminology? (First, that is, after a re-branding in north-east Surrey into the *patois* formula *dun* – we shall shortly address specifically this concept of sequential renamings). The distribution of *stede* (broadly mapped in Figure 3d) might thus show the new language English spreading south from London and the *dun* belt, across estates sitting on the relatively fertile acres of the eastern North Downs plateau and its fringes.

'Estate' or 'farmstead' does seem to be the word. **Banstead** is 'farm where beans are grown'; **Chipstead** we have seen is 'market *stede*'. Such names seem an extension of the agrarian expansionism already noted for **Clandon** (close to **Horsely** and **Sheep Lees**) and **Chaldon**. Are we dealing here with that strengthening rural economy under the stable conditions of Aethelberht of Kent's leadership over southern England around the turn of the seventh century?

In this east Surrey zone we find also farmsteads including **Bedlested** ('*byden stede*', which could refer either to a 'deep valley' or to a 'cistern'), **Alderstead** ('old *stede*', now merely a farm on the Downs) and **Haxted** ('high *stede*', on the edge of the Eden marshes); these look to be later names, in a zone where *stede* remained fashionable. The zone extends into Kent, while a similar phenomenon occurs on the east Hampshire Downs. An 'erratic' (as geographers say) is a mini-set in the Godalming area: **Elstead** ('elder-tree *stede*'), and the non-parish names **Polsted Manor** ('*stede* by a pool', interestingly lying within reach of a Roman villa), **Munstead** (see Chapter 12), a second **Ashstead** and the *hamstede* name **Unstead** (Tuneshamstede in 1241). These too may have been agrarian expansion zones at an early date.

Where does '-ton' come from?

Now here's a strange thing. We have almost completed an entire study, yet said scarcely a thing about *the* most typical of English place-name types, '-ton'. You know: Southampton, Wellington, Burton, Taunton, **Kingston, Sutton.** The fact is, as *Place-Names* says, Surrey is a county with a low proportion of such names. Why? The reason must be that most of Surrey's estate names are *earlier* than the *tun* era, which is accepted as starting rather late, in the late seventh century. But because Surrey learned English very early, being so close to London and being a trendy place, the county once again has the distinction of having some of the country's first *tun* names.

Tun is generally agreed to have carried on being coined for place-names for centuries. Indeed, to have seen off all rivals. The once fashionable formulae *dun, stede, ingas* and *ham* went out of business pretty much as *tun* arrived on the scene. Which is curious, and something not much commented upon. All *tun's* rivals seemingly were born and died within the seventh century (though *patois 'dun'* may be earlier). Odd? Not necessarily so. In fact quite the opposite. All these terms date from the heady days when Celtic and Germanic were vying for the heart of the nation, or at least of London. *Tun* was not used earlier because it did not exist. It was universal after, because it was itself a kind of resolution between British and Anglo-Saxon culture, a resolution the country was ready for only from the later seventh century onwards. I had better explain.

Tun is said to derive from the same root as German *zaun*, 'fence'. This was never a convincing theory. After all, if this were a perfectly normal Anglo-Saxon word, why would it pop up late, and then so dominantly? A more satisfying idea is that *tun*, our 'town', is as with 'downland', a late example of *patois*, and actually arises from *dun*. Circumstantial evidence: in Surrey, *dun* names persistently have transmuted into *tun* – Hertindon veering towards **Artington** by the twelfth century, Cisendune, **Chessington** by the sixteenth and little **Waddington** in Coulsdon the same. This is not strong evidence. But perhaps the *Chronicle* gives sight of the word in gestation; it refers to the four '*tunas*' of Limbury, Aylesbury, Benson and Eynsham captured by Cuthwulf (said to be Caewlin's brother) in 571. John Morris perhaps rightly guesses these places may have been the Anglo-Saxon strongholds of rival *foederati*. Be that as it may, it seems reasonable to me that these *tunas* were what in Wales might have been called *dinas* ('fort'), and slightly earlier in the *patois* of the Vale of Buckingham where these stronghold lie, *dun*. Which is why I say *tun* exemplifies the melding of the two cultures – British *dun*, and English language expansionism – and sweeps all before it. England becoming English.

Sutton (the modern town) may be the earliest recorded use of the formula, again in the Chertsey charter of the 670s. More exciting still, we may have an example of an extant *dun* name surviving alongside a new guise as *tun*. I refer to the parish of **Morden** in the Surrey *dun* belt. Its boundaries suggest it once to have been a piece with the parish of **Merton**; the division could be explained as the result of a single estate split between two new hundreds (Wallington and Brixton) when my putative Tooting hundred went under, conceivably as a result of Mercian activity in the 670s. The two names are essentially the same, the one *patois/patois,* the other English/*patois* : *mor dun* ('marsh *dun*') and *mere tun* ('marsh *tun*'). I am admittedly, improvising. The actual evidence is *Mordune* (969), and *Mertone* (967) with a *Merantune* recorded in the *Chronicle* for 755 which may or may not be the Surrey Merton (but which if it is, could be an example of a corrupted -*an*- formula similar to that seen in 'Crecganford' or indeed perhaps 'Wibbandun'). (Commoner are the Moreton/Morton names of elsewhere, a Gloucester instance being known from 714; this is *mor tun*, a form intermediate between Surrey's versions).

Both the geographical spread of *tun* in Surrey (shown diagrammatically in Figure 3f), and its choice of first-element, back up this notion of cultural fusion. Although *tun* in Surrey is less frequent than in many other counties, it dominates in a swathe of parishes intermixed with or just south of the *dun* zone: **Walton on Thames, Ditton, Merton, Cuddington** (which disappeared when Henry VIII built Nonesuch Palace), **Sutton, Wallington, Beddington, Addington, Walton on the Hill** and **Gatton**. Is this not English-ification, spreading outwards from the *dun* zone? Other *tun* places, further south in Surrey, are virtually all (**Wotton** is an exception) lesser and presumably later-named sites that seem to fill-in between existing estate names. Perhaps these are hamlets and farms reflecting population growth. **Newington Butts** by Walworth is nicely illustrative, being 'new *tun*/farmstead' (the butts refer to archery, in case you were wondering). Other examples include

Santon and **Littleton** manors in Reigate, **Sutton** manor in Woking, and **Sutton** hamlet in Shere. In the far south-west *tun* is rare, but we find two **Compton**'s and another **Littleton** in the Godalming area.

Equally, *tun*'s first-elements are redolent of cultural melding. There are personal-names reminiscent of *ham* names, usually in the formula -*ingtun* : **Cuddington, Beddington, Addington.** Then there are 'site' names as with *stede* : **Walton on the Hill** ('wall'), **Ditton** ('dyke'), **Merton** ('marsh'). There are even 'folk' names, notably *weala tun* (see next chapter). But most typical are 'location' or diminutive names including **Sutton** ('south'), **Weston** ('west'), **Milton** ('middle') and **Littleton** (guess!) that by any definition imply subservience to, or at least later arrival than, an existing nearby estate name. But with *tun* we become English, whatever our prior history.

Celtic survival in west Surrey

One little detail I have missed out: the 'nature names' of west Surrey. Their generalized distribution is indicated in Figure 3f. This category embraces the parish names **Shere, Send, Ash, Shalford, Pyrford, Wonersh, Pirbright, Wanborough** and **Byfleet.** They don't conform to any of the normal formulations, and spurn twiddly endings, or else utilise *patois* or uncommon ones.

Kenneth Rutherford Davis was perhaps right when he wrote of the Chilterns, that 'nature names' were *direct translations from the Celtic.* The same may be true of west Surrey. Celtic culture survived in such areas until late; archaeologists say so.

Now, I cannot prove to you that **Shere**, or rather **Sherbourne**, had originally a Celtic name meaning the same thing, but it is likely. I think I can prove it for **Crooksbury** because this is a rare example of a twiddly-bit being added to explain, accurately as it happens, the original Celtic : *cruc beorg* being 'barrow-barrow'. And the remarkable survival of purely Celtic **Merrow** ('marly ground') pretty likely was paralleled not far away by an original Celtic name later translated as **Send** ('sandy ground'). By the same token, a name like **Ash** looks to be from the same stable as the Celtic element *limen*, 'elm', in **Limpsfield.**

Byfleet ('by the river'), **Wonersh** (perhaps 'crooked field'), **Shalford** ('shallow ford'), **Wanborough** ('white', or 'wagon barrow'?), **Hambledon** ('crooked hill'), **Hascombe** ('witch's valley') are the sort of meanings you might find in a scatter of still-Celtic names in Wales. And of course the commonest handle, the archetypal Surrey '-ley' as in

Frimley, etc. may not be a twiddly-bit either. Whether Celtic-derived or not, it is not so much a linguistic add-on as a socially-relevant description of a chunk of public territory in the Welsh manner.

That these Celtic foundations once extended across the whole of Surrey is shown by similarities between some west Surrey 'nature names' and some east Surrey place-names blessed with twiddly-bits. As we have seen, for **Send** read **Sanderstead**, etc. For **Ash**, **Ashtead**. But counter-intuitively, Send and Ash may have been translated into English *later* than Sanderstead or Ashstead.

Local centres of English-ification, and anomalies explained

So, let us assume a hybrid form of Low German language, concocted from a mixture of the Jutish of Aethelberht, the Anglian of Raedwald and Oswald, the Saxon of Wessex and the Frisian of London's principal foreign traders. (Jutland and Angeln were parts of Denmark, Saxony the German coast, and Frisia is coastal Holland. Whether their pre-migration peoples spoke tongues noticeably different from each other is a question, but certainly the various Anglo-Saxon kingdoms had marked linguistic distinctions, which to some extent persist to the present.) Within 200 years this hybrid becomes the *lingua franca* of local ruling families, of the re-emerging metropolis of the port of London, and of the Latin-speaking metropolitan ecclesiastical communities of Canterbury, York and St Paul's. Because of the early economic and cultural dominance of heavily-Germanised East Anglia (to which most of the population of Angeln is said to have emigrated), the term eventually adopted for this *lingua franca* was 'English', that is Anglian. A name which Bede, Northumbrian Angle as he was (and whose book in ecclesiastical Latin *A History of the English Church and People* became immensely influential throughout the literate Church), disingenuously applied to the collective peoples of eastern Britain. We became 'Angleland', England; but probably only because we gave up Celtic. Otherwise we would still be Celto-Latin 'Britannia', Britain. (Which, courtesy of the 1704 Act of Union, we still are, in parallel of course to being England).

Commercial London was perhaps the main source of the English language, with Canterbury a good second. Perhaps Mercian Kingston too, as Mercian royalty regarded itself as Anglian. But language does not spread like wine across the tablecloth of a nation; it jumps from king to king, poseur to poseur, central place to central place, fair to farm, as does any new fashion. In his thatched manor-house in Cobham or wherever the local lord will want to display London fashions to his local subordinates. Lowly peasants, Britons many of them, won't be part of this for a while.

How do we know what language the lord of Cobham – if there was one – spoke, and when? Place-name distributions may come to our aid.

Geographers love spatial anomalies: distributions that buck the trend. If English did spread out from London, and take a couple of centuries or more to reach the extremities of the county, then we have problems. One is the occurrence of 'nature names' right up close to London: **Sheen** (the old name for Richmond, and meaning either 'beautiful' or 'sheds', take your pick), **Barnes** (sounds like 'barns'), **Mortlake** (one explanation of which is 'salmon meadow') and ones already noted, **Kew** and **Camberwell**. We don't know the origin date of any of these names, though I have suggested the last two to be pagan; but if they reflect once-Celtic names it would be not too surprising. The immediate London area was *not* one of the very early Germanic settlement zones. London was politically 'British'.

Equally fascinating territory for the place-name specialist is the linguistically anarchic situation on the eastern North Downs as indicated by Figure 3. Although I have presented *dun, stede, ham* and *tun* have been presented as discrete fashion-events tied to discrete polities and identifiable geographical zones, all neatness disappears up on the Downs. The fashions are jumbled into a mixed bag of parish names in the most impolite manner: **Coulsdon, Chaldon, Sanderstead, Banstead, Chipstead, Chelsham, Woldingham, Warlingham, Addington, Gatton**. Yet all are pretty similar places, just plateau farmlands; you could swap any of their twiddly bits around and no-one would notice the difference (try Chipham, Woldingdon...). It's a mess. Which of course precisely illustrates my point. *There is no difference of meaning – they are simply linguistic fashions.* They are scrambled up here, because this being the grain basket of the region, every Tom, Dick and Hereward has tramped through and dumped their particular linguistic predilection. It's the penalty for economic success.

What might be called 'The Godalming Anomaly' is as enlightening (see Figures 3d and 3f). Here, way out in the sticks, we stumble across a remarkable collection of place-name types, some of which shouldn't be there. Apart from a couple of *ingas* names and a couple of pagan ones, there are the *stede* names that should be in east Surrey. There are an awful lot of *patois* names in *ford* and *cumb,* too: **Ockford, Milford** ('mill'), **Shackleford** (undeciphered), **Oxenford** (just like Oxford),

Tilford (either 'Tilla's' or 'convenient'), two **Compton's**, **Farncombe** ('bracken') and **Binscombe** (perhaps another *byden* name). *Cumb* is dialect 'coomb/combe', Celtic-derived, and a parallel to Welsh *cwm*,'valley'; but since these places in the Godalming area are *not* in abrupt coomb-like valleys, may be 'British valley settlement', equivalent but subsequent to *dun,* and arising in safer times (whereas further away names like **Thorncombe**, **Nurscombe** and **Highcombe Bottom** really are valleys, suggesting *cumb* subsequently reverted to its original meaning).

My guess is that the regionally important temple of Peper Harow and the *Burghal Hidage* fortress of Eashing reflect a politically important territory – perhaps a Wealden mini-kingdom – pagan and Celtic, hanging on from the Roman villa culture of Compton and Chiddingfold, which turned about and enthusiastically absorbed the new 'English' culture. The ostentatious Germanicism of the god-names Tiw and Tunor at Tuesley and Thursley does not detract from such a scenario. As Nicholas Higham has said, one would expect canny British leaders to take up new Germanic gods, the latter being so obviously better at war-mongering. Pagan still-Celtic Caedwalla crashed through here in the 680s, but by then he was in the minority among the local nobility. English was here to stay.

This putative anthropological detail is essential to the big picture. Tore Janson, theorist of national *lingua francas*, has not, apparently, appreciated that his theories apply happily to southern England. Janson reckons it takes 200 to 400 years for a national language to change, and that the moving forces are usually the institutions of religion, education, the military and trade. For Surrey in the seventh century read: the Church, the Church again, the Heptarchy, and London. (The concept is straightforward enough if I simply mention the latest 'culture' – Americanisation – to swash out in waves from London. '*Plus ça change…*').

The tidemarks of language history

It's time to draw together the various theories scattered throughout this book. We can explain a good half of Surrey's parish names – including those carrying *dun, stede, ham* and *tun* – as the tidemarks of language history written across the face of the county. The tidemarks of successive linguistic fashions, charted through space and time. If we throw in also names with pre-Germanic elements, *ge, ingas, feld* and *wudu*, then the claim of 'a good half' becomes tenable.

My findings are summarized in Figure 3, where Surrey's place-name types are shown as aspects of successive political influences visited upon the county. My model of a neat series of formula changes associated with distinct eras of outside pressure, is of course over-simplified. But that's what models are: over-simplifications, adopted simply in order to see the wood for the trees.

However, there is one sensitive little matter still to discuss. I've probably left enough clues scattered throughout this book. In the specifics of place-name studies, it arises as the question of *who* named each place-name, and what their relationship might have been to the rest of the local community.

14. The ceorls of Charlwood

The meaning of place-names cannot be detached from the issue of who did the naming. Which leads to a rather fundamental question, namely: *Who were the English?*

I have not read the surviving Kent and Wessex law codes, apparently with their divisions of society into complex social hierarchies and explicit Anglo- Saxon and British cadres (though I know they exist). I *have* read Bede where he mentions in passing that Wilfrid freed 200 slaves from the royal estate he was gifted at Selsey. Rival Anglo-Saxon groups quite happily sold prisoners-of-war (including other Anglo-Saxons) into slavery, as Pope Gregory noticed. The Romanised Brits knew a thing or two about slavery too – their villa system probably depended upon them, and elements of this system may have continued. But it is not just about slaves.

Lessons from anthropology

Place-name studies traditionally have been something of an anthropology-free zone. For example, a common assumption is that because a scribe writes down a place-name in English, then the place *is* English, or even English-speaking. This in spite of the Creechbarrow evidence.

Personal-names have been presumed to define race. Yet I myself have a Scottish Gaelic first name, though I am not Scottish. We know that fairly quickly after 1066 everyone (or at least, anyone who was anyone) seemed to be going around with a Norman Christian-name. Was England suddenly populated by Normans? Improbable. Doubtless a similar thing happened after 43 AD when the Roman legions arrived with *their* exotic personal-names. And doubtless too, after 410 AD when the Saxons officially arrived.

And then there are those Germanic gods. If Thunderfield, Thursley and Tuesley celebrate Germanic gods, are the locals necessarily Germanic, or even *all* of them Germanic? If my eldest son takes up Buddhism tomorrow, is he Tibetan?

Cultures are commodities. They travel, and are distinct from the individuals they affect. Sometimes they *seem* to disappear, as when

Roman industrialized goods ceased economic production; but of course they do not entirely disappear.

The Men of Holmesdale who Never Wonne

The *Anglo-Saxon Chronicle* is a thoroughly biased document. During the ninth century it is quite up front about the military prowess of our home team, the 'Men of Surrey'. These are presented as on a par with the men of Sussex and of Kent. We are even given the name of one of their leaders: Huda.

Were I a romantic I would have no hesitation in identifying these proud warriors as direct descendants of the first Anglo-Saxons whose communities gave us the early cemeteries at Mitcham and Croydon. In John Morris' terms, they were Germanic mercenaries who came to dominate the London region, notably in the persons of Ceawlin and Cuthwulf in the later sixth century.

However, as an old boy of Reigate Grammar School I am an inheritor also of some shadowy characters called in our school motto 'The Men of Holmesdale', who apparently 'Never wonne ne never shall'. It seems this did not mean they were bad at rugger and never won. Rather, they were never *beaten* and never would be. Nobody knew, in my day, who these people were, or what war they fought in, and nobody does now.

Aclea, somewhere in or near Surrey, is recorded by the *Chronicle* as a great victory against invading Danes in 851. **Oakley Wood** near Merstham is now largely flattened by the M25/M23 interchange but is not far from the interestingly named **Battlebridge**. (Other candidates for Aclea are Oakley in Hants, **Ockley Common** near Godalming in west Surrey, and **Ockley** in the Surrey Weald, but we won't worry about that). Oakley Wood lies, or lay, in the Vale of Holmesdale that stretches east to what is now Kent. The vale of the *Celtic* place-names **Limpsfield** and Chevening. Which does raise the possibility that the *Chronicle's* Men of Surrey were a mixed bunch of conscripts: some tall Germanic types from Mitcham, and some Britons from the Vale. Just like the normal rugger match.

Brits and Anglo's

The matter of race is strenuously avoided in polite society. 'Twas not always so. Place-name study caught the backend of Victorian racism and adopted a thoroughly Germanist approach to the interpretation of England's place-name heritage. There was little thought that some elements might be Celtic, as Celtic was unfashionable at the time (for Celtic read: Fenian rebels in Ireland). Also, many of the principal early place-name scholars were Germanic-speakers, based in universities in Germany or Scandinavia, and the discipline is still living with the consequences. (My own academic hero is Eilert Ekwall, a Swede from Lund).

Race is no longer fashionable, but our grandfathers were less squeamish and as a result collected some interesting evidence. Worth citing in full is a passage by Charles Kingsley, quoted in Eric Parker's *Highways and Byways in Surrey* (1904). Talking of the people of the Surrey/Sussex/Hants borderlands, he writes:

'The clod [*sic*] of these parts is the descendent of many generations of broom squires and deer stealers; the instinct of sport is strong within him still, though no more of the Queen's deer are to be shot in the winter turnip fields, or worse, caught by an apple-baited hook hung from an orchard bough. He now limits his aspirations to hares and pheasants, and too probably once in his life 'hits the keeper into the river', and reconsiders himself for a while over a crank in Winchester gaol. Well, he has his faults, and I have mine. But he is a thoroughly good fellow nevertheless. Civil, contented, industrious, and often very handsome; a far shrewder fellow too – owing to his dash of wild forest blood from gipsey, highwayman, and what not – than his bullet-headed and flaxen-polled cousin, the pure South Saxon of the chalk downs. Dark-haired he is, and ruddy, and tall of bone; swaggering in his youth: but when he grows old a thorough gentleman, reserved, stately, and courteous as a prince...'

Such evidence is of uncertain value, but the contrast between dark Wealden folk and the fair South Saxon is striking (though, as in western Ireland where dark features have been attributed to 'Spaniards shipwrecked from the Armada', so Kingsley calls upon 'gipsy' blood). Lingering racial differences would not be impossible, as is thought to be the case in the dark-haired people still found in the land of the Silures in Gwent. And this after centuries of what geneticists call socially-enforced 'differential breeding advantage'.

Equivalent evidence could hardly be collected in Surrey today. Most broom squires have perhaps moved to housing estates in Basingstoke or Guildford, and the county inter-shuffled with immigrants from further afield (including my own grandparents from Cumbria and the Fens).

Wealh and *weallisc*

I have blithely assumed that *wealh* refers to 'British-speakers', because this seems to me a logical reading. But there are other overtones too. *Weala tun* names are strongly suggestive of the *ceorla tun* names (Charlton/Chorlton) which seem to have superseded them, and which likewise take the form of subsidiary settlements close to main centres of local power. One is obliged to consider whether the *wealh* did not simply become the *ceorl* : the 'welsh' became the 'free peasant'. The only Surrey example of a *ceorl* parish name is **Charlwood** by Thunderfield. The distinction between *wealh* and *ceorl* could be that in their formative years the *ceorl* spoke 'Welsh', that is British. Such place-names mark a phase in the transition from a national Celtic to a national Germanic language. On the evidence of the *weala tun* place-names, this change was occurring in Surrey during the late seventh century.

But as David Crystal might point out, 'standard' English would vary by locality and by era, *but also by class.* Hitherto unmentioned evidence of this process might be found in the Weald. In the country south of Dorking and Reigate where the forest lingered long and *wudu* names are found, occur also several names in *wealisc*. These include thirteenth-century surnames and place-names seemingly reflective of them: Waleys, **Waley's Farm**, **Wallis Gill** (all in Ockley parish), and Waley, **Walliswood** (in the south of Abinger parish). Do such names imply an influx of Welsh people at some date in history? That seems rather far-fetched. More likely they record the late survival, and subsequent memory of British-speaking in this relatively remote area.

And yes it gives me great pleasure to think that as a boy, paddling about in the Wally Brook beyond the edge of town, I was partaking in a little bit of history. The official name of this stream across which we built dams and upon which we floated our lit bangers in empty matchboxes is the **Wallace Brook** – identical perhaps to the Walbrook, and another *wealisc* marker.

Cotmen and ceorls

The lasting cultural continuity is the relationship with the land; the relationship of the *community* with the land. It is a relationship we are in danger of losing, if we have not lost it already. Which is why I personally am a member of the Surrey Wildlife Trust as well as the Surrey Archaeological Society. We have a collective responsibility to our future.

Charlwood has been cited. I do not know who the 'ceorls' were, and historians are confusing as to whether ceorls were relatively high status individuals (the free housecarls who joined with local nobles in bashing up rivals), or of lowly status ('churlish' peasants). Were they emergent yeomen, with a hundred or more acres as at Waley's Farm? Or were they the medieval 'cotmen' with five acres and a cottage? (There is still today a Cotland Farm in Charlwood, or at least *Place-Names* says there is, though it may be under a runway).

Charlwood's companions are names like **Cotmandene** in Dorking: 'the valley of the cotmen'. Cotmen were the Domesday Book's cottars, the cottagers, some of whom presumably lived in sundry Surrey hamlets called **Woodcote**; **Westcott** appears in the *Book* itself. The various strata of society overlapped, were defined, redefined, and finally almost disappeared. This was the feudal system, a possible Roman (or indeed Bronze Age) hangover which succumbed only to the enclosures of the common lands during our extended Agrarian and Industrial Revolutions, or at least, was transmuted to a more fluid urban version.

But tenacious social layerings hide a more solid history of social endeavour: the collective management of local resources. Did the cotmen of Dorking *collectively manage* their valley? Similarly, did the ceorls collectively manage their wood at Charlwood, and their meadow at the lost Cotman meade in Merstham? Equivalent names existed in the parishes of Barnes, Chertsey, Egham and Lambeth; Merstham had also a Towneman meade (now **Townsend Meads**), where 'townman' is parishioner.

One might imagine that Anglo-Saxon and medieval ceorls and cotmen were all little individualists, or else all tied labour. Probably some were and some weren't. I have mislaid my copy of Wilfrid Hooper's *Reigate, Its Story Through the Ages,* but remember the seventeenth-century regulations (I think it was seventeenth) relating to **Earlswood Common**, my local common. These defined who could cut the herbage, and presumably graze their geese, ducks or goats, when and in what quantity. It is remarkable that such a system survived through the ages. One thinks it must have originated in the early years of agriculture, or at least the early days of significant population density. Certainly they were not dreamed up by the earl. Equivalent rules – and they are commoners' rights as much as landowner's laws – still define the use of the common today, now applied by the democratic Borough of Reigate and Banstead, ensuring for example that my parents and their neighbours don't cut down all the trees for fuel this winter. Without such rules, collectively derived, agreed and enforced, the common would be a dead duck. So would we all.

The namers

Only now, with these last two chapters, when we have faced up to the matters of language change and of social class, can we even hope to answer the question of *who* named any particular place-name. Which after all is a fairly important question. How can we guess what a place-name meant if we have no idea who named it or for what purpose?

I have implied several namers in action over the years.

Priests would have named a **Woking** or a **Godalming** – the club names of proud aristocratic households-*cum*-monasteries, on a par with Bede's Tunnacastir and Maldulfi urbs.

Land agents (usually again monastic) would have systematized the estate names of the minsters' territories, embracing a 'Cofa's *ham*' and an 'Ebba's *ham*'. We do not know what these estates' previous names were (well, we do for **Cobham** – Getinges – though that again was only a temporary moniker).

Which agencies systematized the *dun* and *stede* names we do not know, though one might guess that the Eldorman Aelfred knows something about the *feld* names. And whence the '-ley' names – local community parlance? Ditto **Shere**, *a.k.a.* **Sherbourne**? Or 'Limp', before the Eldorman got to it? We don't actually know. By whose mistake was **Merrow** recorded, when it would otherwise have been translated into English? To be frank, your guess is as good as mine. But without having a stab at who named what and when, meanings will remain elusive.

15. To conclude

Some rather radical reinterpretations have been made in this book. Reinterpretations indeed of a whole series of familiar and less familiar early place-name types, most notably those containing the Old English elements *leah, feld, wudu, hamm, ham, cruc, wielle, ge, ingas, eg,* some *burh,* and *hoh.* This can be seen to be the result largely of the paradigms put forward at the beginning, which appear to have stood up to testing.

My own estimate is that hitherto, place-names studies have paid insufficient attention to several crucial aspects, namely:

- ⊕ the role of *religion,*
- ⊕ the role of *social class,*
- ⊕ *cultural continuity,*
- ⊕ *function* (as opposed to *place),*
- ⊕ the importance of regional *politics,*
- ⊕ the *migration of place-names* with estate activity centres,
- ⊕ the resultant *clusters of relict central-place names,*
- ⊕ the *influence of London,* and
- ⊕ the long-winded change from Celtic to English as our national *lingua franca.*

If I am right, then some interesting conclusions follow.

Place-names and archaeology

Archaeologists and place-name students have fallen out of late. Rob Poulton has gone so far as to say that at least for west Surrey, archaeology and place-name studies come up with completely different views as to the history of these parts, and therefore one of them must be wrong. We can now say with confidence that it is the place-name interpretations that have been wrong, which is one good reason for producing this book. Place-name study can now offer a real contribution to archaeology and to social history.

Some place-name elements may be directly translatable into proxies for archaeological sites (always bearing in mind that the name may have migrated). *Cruc* indicates a prehistoric barrow; *beorg* a prehistoric or Anglo-Saxon barrow. *Cader* seems to be a prehistoric hill fort; *burh* either a prehistoric hill fort, an Anglo-Saxon fort, an early monastic enclosure, a town, a manor or a suburb. *Llys* a post-Roman court. *Stret* is usually an engineered Roman road (though newer names may simply be a modern 'street'); *hyth* a significant quay or harbour. Both *ford* and *brycg* can be causeways (though the latter subsequently a bridge).

Ingas I have associated with mid-seventh century royal monasteries, and perhaps *waru* too. (One of the meanings of another parallel element, *folk*, is 'people of the diocese', as Tom Williamson confirms for 'Norfolk' and 'Suffolk'). *Eg* in major names is an early monastery; *hearg* and *weoh* pagan temples; *ecles* a British church. *Ge* relates to early ecclesiastical administrative areas; *hoh* to hundredal origins; *plegstow, stow* and *falod* to a variety of social gathering-places; and *ora* to extremely venerable meeting-places. In the minutiae of pagan tradition I have suggested specific roles for *funta, wielle* and *caeg*, as well as some *hamm* and perhaps *stapol*.

Regarding the history of landscape I have identified *leah* with common-land grazing, *hyrst* with coppice, *ritu* with native river-crossings. *Ham* relates to early estates.

Place-names and cultural history

Agrarian and ecological history, economic and mercantile history, religious history, political, social and cultural history in their widest sense, are subjects normally kept well apart. Their various specialists scarcely speak to one another. Similarly, the schools of Romano-British, Anglo-Saxon, medieval and modern historians scarcely speak to each other. But place-names are wonderfully integrative.

That one place-name **Limpsfield** conjures up an awful lot. Primeval elms, the River Eden, a sacred spring in Titsey park, a Roman road, a Romano-British temple. A putative lost monastery (as much to do with the name **Titsey**), an estate with its 'field', our parish church and village. And the passage of English across the face of Surrey. All wrapped up in a single name. Surely, a veritable feast for the intellectual palate?

Further research

I will have made mistakes in my analyses. But if even a half of the models of place-name and place-name element meanings proposed in this book are valid, then our understanding of the 'Dark Ages' in Surrey will have been significantly improved. Hopefully, other researchers will check my results, and also take a similar approach for other counties to see if they are part of a wider pattern.

Archaeology may help. I look forward, for example, to traces of an Anglo-Saxon causeway being discovered at Tilford, and a seventh century minster being found under St Martin's parish church in Dorking. But of course, if it existed, it may lie elsewhere.

Useful reading

The local database is *The Place-Names of Surrey*, compiled by the English Place-Name Society in 1934. For the nationwide picture my favourites remain Eilert Ekwall's *The Concise Oxford Dictionary of English Place-Names* (4th edition 1960), and A. Rivet and C. Smith's *The Place-Names of Roman Britain* (1979).

Specific place-names studies cited in this book are: Barrie Cox's 'The place-names of the earliest English records' (*EPNS Journal 8*, 1976), Richard Coates' 'Methodological reflections on Leatherhead' (*EPNS Journal 12*, 1980), Joan Wakeford in *Surrey Archaeological Society Collections 75* (1984), Kenneth Cameron's 'The meaning and significance of Old English *walh* in English place-names' (*EPNS Journal 12*, 1980), Margaret Gelling's *Signposts to the Past* (1988), and Gillian Fellows-Jensen's 'Place-names as a reflection of cultural interaction' (*Anglo-Saxon England 19*, 1990). Margaret Gelling and Ann Cole's *The Landscape of Place-Names* (2000) has good compilations classified by suffix, though we differ on meanings.

If you are brave enough to attempt your own investigations into the way words are formed and change meaning you will need R.J. Clark Hall's *A Concise Anglo-Saxon Dictionary* (4th edition 1960), J. Pokorny's *Indogermanisches Etymological Worterbuch* (4th edition 2002), and the notes on word origins in *The Concise Oxford Dictionary*. You might also seek out a text on Welsh word origins. But for a serious attempt at understanding word meanings you will need to read far more widely.

The contemporary documentation consists principally of the *Anglo-Saxon Chronicle* (e.g. the Pheonix Press edition of 2000), Bede (e.g. Penguin 1968), *Beowulf* (e.g. Penguin 1995) and for Celtic insights the *Mabinogion* (e.g. Dent 1989). For the early charters I have relied on *The Place-Names of Surrey* and to a lesser extent Blair (1991, see below).

Thereafter, your notions will be much affected by your subsequent choice of reading. First, archaeology. The Surrey data has been analysed by the Surrey Archaeological Society in its volumes *The Archaeology of Surrey to 1540* (1987) and *Aspects of Archaeology and*

History in Surrey (2004), to one or other of which the researchers I cite (Poulton, Bird, Hines, Macphail and Scaife) have contributed. On the fascinating issue of Roman roads get a feel from R. Chevalier's *Roman Roads* (1976), but also Oliver Rackham (see below).

John Blair's perspective as an historian may be consulted in *Early Medieval Surrey: Landholding, Church and Settlement* (SAS, 1991), though his discussion of Surrey *ingas* place-names in Stephen Bassett's, *The Origins of the Anglo-Saxon Kingdoms* (1989) is to my mind misleading. For useful comparisons with other territories see Alan Everitt's *Continuity and Colonisation: the Evolution of Kentish Settlement* (1986), Kenneth Rutherford Davis's *Britons and Saxons: the Chiltern region 400-700* (1982), and Tom Williamson's, *The Origins of Norfolk* (1993). Peter Brandon's *The South Saxons* (1978) is perhaps too steeped in the old paradigms to be overly handy; try rather Barry Cunliffe's *The Regni* (1973).

For English history as wider theatre try Frank Stenton's *Anglo-Saxon England* (1971), and D.J. Fisher's *The Anglo-Saxon Age* (1973) for its ecclesiastical perspective. But for the new paradigm you will need John Morris's *The Age of Arthur: A History of the British Isles from 350 to 650* (1973), Michael Wood's *Domesday, A Search for England* (1986), and the works of Nicholas Higham (*Rome, Britain and the Anglo-Saxons,* 1992; *An English Empire,* 1995; *The Convert Kings,* 1997). The outcome in 'pre-industrial', pre-suburban Surrey is visible in Daniel Defoe's *A Tour Through the Whole Island of Great Britain* (published over 1724–26), and William Cobbett's *Rural Rides* (published 1830, reprinted Penguin 2001). However, from all the above one gleans that Surrey has been partially industrial and partially suburban these 2,000 years.

On Surrey's urban archaeology see also M. O'Connell and R. Poulton, 'The towns of Surrey' in J. Haslam (ed.) *Anglo-Saxon Towns in Southern England,* 1984; and on London's see T. Dyson and J. Schofield chapter in Haslam. On Surrey's ecology a standard text is J.E. Lousley's *Flora of Surrey* (1976). On the landscape, and specifically the history of woodland, see Oliver Rackham's *The History of the Countryside* (1986).

Surrey folklore data is thin, but antiquarian John Aubrey's reports were gathered in the late seventh century and Martin Tupper's inventions embroidered in the nineteenth; an easy introduction may be gleaned from Eric Parker's *Highways and Byways in Surrey* (1908, revised 1935).

For some feeling as to how pre-Germanic pagan traditions operated in England and the possible extent of their continuity I have had to go to an Irish researcher, Daithi O'Hogain of University College Dublin and his *The Sacred Isle: Belief and Religion in Pre-Christian Ireland* (1999), and to a Continental one with C. Eluere's *The Celts: First Masters of Europe* (1993). Material on Anglo-Saxon (and come to that, British) paganism is fashionable in some quarters though not always academically respectable, but try Tony Linsell's *Anglo-Saxon Mythology* (1994).

Only once you have absorbed this little lot is it worth returning to an analysis of Surrey's place-name meanings, though not before making a necessary excursion into current advances in social linguistics. Try H. Hoijer's 'The Relation of Language to Culture' (*American Anthropological Association Memoir No. 79*, 1962), P. Sims-Williams' 'Genetics, Linguistics and Pre-History' (*Antiquity*, vol. 72, no. 277, 1998), Tore Jansen's *Speak: A Short History of Languages* (2002), David Crystal's *The Stories of English* (2004) and on language and class, anything you can find by Basil Bernstein.

You are now in a position to test out my explanatory models (undoubtedly some of them will be wrong), and perhaps come up with improved versions. Useful background for the purpose I have found Richard Chorley and Peter Haggett's *Models in Geography* (1967), D.J. Clarke's *Models in Archaeology* (1972), and a little book by another of my former tutors at Bristol, Michael Chisholm's *Rural Settlement and land Use* (1962).

Happy reading.

Index

Latin- or Celtic-derived elements are given in **_bold italic_**.

Germanic terms in _italic_

Also from Heart of Albion Press

How to Write and Publish Local and Family History Successfully

Bob Trubshaw

How to Write and Publish Local and Family History Successfully guides even complete novices through all the stages needed to produce and promote books, booklets, magazines, CD-ROMs and Web sites on local and family history. For those who are not novices the information will also act as a checklist for producing professional-looking publications.

Topics include:

- good writing style
- design and typesetting
- preparing illustrations for reproduction
- estimating costs and cover price
- preparing publicity
- selling to shops
- creating effective Web sites and CD-ROMs

It all adds up to 280 large format pages of advice, references, useful addresses, tips and hints.

All the information is based on Bob Trubshaw's fifteen years of experience publishing local and family history books, booklets, magazines, CD-ROMs and Web sites.

> 'Here's a book that satisfies a real need, magnificently. [...] a well-organised guide, using simple language [...] I have often fielded phone calls from would-be authors and publishers and wished that I could recommend just one book capable of answering all their queries. Now I can.'
> Peter Watson *Family Tree Magazine*

ISBN 1 872883 59 1. April 2005. 245 x 175 mm, 262 + xviii pages, 32 b&w illustrations, paperback. **£16.95**

Understanding Leicestershire and Rutland Place-Names

Jill Bourne

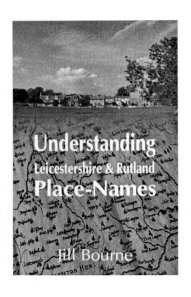

We take for granted the names we use for places. Yet these names are a valuable part of our cultural heritage, providing a detailed insight into the early history of the region. Place-names reveal the otherwise lost voices of our forebears who settled here.

Understanding Leicestershire and Rutland Place-Names analyses the whole range of place-names which occur in Leicestershire and Rutland, most of which were coined between 1,000 and 1,500 years ago. These place-names describe, often in fine detail, the landscape, geology, rivers, buildings, flora, fauna, boundaries, meeting places, roads and track-ways. This book also looks at the distribution of the names, the languages from which they are derived, the successive waves of conquerors and migrants who fought and settled here, and the society they created.

Jill Bourne is an historian, archaeologist and museum professional who has specialised in the area of place-name studies and landscape history for over 20 years.

ISBN 1872883 71 0. Published 2003, perfect bound. Demy 8vo (215 x 138 mm), 145 + viii pages, 5 maps. **£6.95**

Local Surrey author

Explore Fairy Traditions

Jeremy Harte

We are not alone. In the shadows of our countryside there lives a fairy race, older than humans, and not necessarily friendly to them. For hundreds of years, men and women have told stories about the strange people, beautiful as starlight, fierce as wolves, and heartless as ice. These are not tales for children. They reveal the fairies as a passionate, proud, brutal people.

Explore Fairy Traditions draws on legends, ballads and testimony from throughout Britain and Ireland to reveal what the fairies were really like. It looks at changelings, brownies, demon lovers, the fairy host, and abduction into the Otherworld. Stories and motifs are followed down the centuries to reveal the changing nature of fairy lore, as it was told to famous figures like W.B. Yeats and Sir Walter Scott. All the research is based on primary sources and many errors about fairy tradition are laid to rest.

Jeremy Harte combines folklore scholarship with a lively style to show what the presence of fairies meant to people's lives. Like their human counterparts, the secret people could kill as well as heal. They knew marriage, seduction, rape and divorce; they adored some children and rejected others. If we are frightened of the fairies, it may be because their world offers an uncomfortable mirror of our own.

'*Explore Fairy Traditions* is an excellent introduction to the folklore of fairies, and I would highly recommend it.' Paul Mason *Silver Wheel*

ISBN 1 872883 61 3. Published 2004. Demy 8vo (215 x 138 mm), 171 + vi pages, 6 line drawings, paperback. **£9.95**

Also from Heart of Albion Press

Masterworks

Arts and Crafts of Traditional Building in Northern Europe

Nigel Pennick

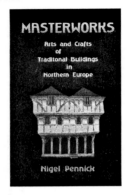

Masterworks is about the traditions of arts and crafts in northern Europe, taking as a starting point the use of timber in building. Timber frame buildings have been constructed over a long period of time over a large territory, mostly northern and north-west Europe. Various regional and local styles have come into being.

Timber buildings display a rich diversity of techniques, forms and patterns developed by generations of master craftsmen working with local materials under similar limitations. The 'arts and crafts' used in the construction of these buildings acknowledge and celebrate the knowledge, traditions, abilities and spiritual understanding of how to work effectively with natural materials. They are living traditions that remain relevant today.

Masterworks is a celebration of this arts and crafts ethos that is present in the traditional buildings of northern Europe.

> "*Masterworks* ... is written by a man who is not only in tune with his subject matter but is, in fact, a master wordsmith in his own right and deserves credit for this. I personally found this one of his most intriguing and important works to date and cannot recommend it too highly to the discerning reader."
>
> Ian Read *Runa*

ISBN 1 872883 63 X   Published 2002. Perfect bound, Demy 8vo, 163 + viii pages, 23 b&w photos, 15 line drawings   **£9.95**